A Debut at the Met

A Debut at the Met

by ROBERTA PETERS

with LOUIS BIANCOLLI

MEREDITH PRESS • New York

First edition

Library of Congress Catalog Card Number: 67-26179

MANUFACTURED IN THE UNITED STATES OF AMERICA FOR MEREDITH PRESS

VAN REES PRESS • NEW YORK

Foreword

ONE of the most spectacular Met debuts of my time was that of Roberta Peters as Zerlina in Mozart's *Don Giovanni* on November 17, 1950. Totally unknown and inexperienced, having been on the stage only once—when she was auditioning for a place on the Met roster—and never having sung an opera performance in public or even rehearsed with the company, her appearance as a last-minute replacement for the indisposed Nadine Conner was a triumph.

Who was this girl, where did she come from? There must be a story to explain the story of that exciting night, I thought. So I hurried backstage to find out. The chronicle that follows is the authentic step-by-step account in Miss Peters' own style, with anecdotes and dialogue just as she remembered them, of what preceded that dramatic debut. This is the first time, to my knowledge, that the story *before* the career has been told: the young dream, the hard work, the determination that bring the artist to the threshold of fame. This story is just as it happened, just as Miss Peters recounted it to me, and it ends as she ended it: "And I walked out."

Louis Biancolli

Cast

ROBERTA PETERS (*née* Peterman) .... Metropolitan Soprano

RUTH PETERMAN .... Mother

SOL PETERMAN .... Father

LEON HIRSCH .... Grandfather

JAN PEERCE .... Metropolitan Tenor

WILLIAM HERMAN .... Voice Teacher

SOL HUROK .... Concert Manager

MAE FROHMAN .... Assistant to Sol Hurok

RUDOLF BING .... General Manager of the Met

MAX RUDOLF .... Assistant Manager and Conductor

HERBERT GRAF .... Stage Director

FRITZ REINER .... Conductor

MARGARET CARSON .... Press Director of the Met

ANTONIETTA STABILE .... Teacher of Italian and Dramatics

"UNCLE HARRY" .... Voice Teacher

HENRY SMITH .... Piano Accompanist

ESTELLE .... A Friend

OBSERVER AND AMANUENSIS .... Louis Biancolli

Contents

A Debut at the Met

1

♪♪♪♪♪♪♪♪♪♪♪

"I'd Like to Sing at the Metropolitan"

Age: 13

WHILE I was attending P.S. 64 in the Bronx I had a friend named Edna—not my closest friend, but a good friend and a girl I looked up to because she was the only one I knew who was taking singing lessons. Like me, Edna was then about ten years old. I never met anyone who loved to sing as much as Edna did. She sang at home, in school, at parties, everywhere; and she sang everything—songs, bits of arias, hymns, anthems, Negro spirituals. I was different. I sang only at home and my repertory consisted of "Oh, Susanna!" "My Old Kentucky Home," snatches of a few other songs, and practically every commercial jingle on the radio. Complete songs didn't interest me much. A nice, punchy two-liner was more in my line. We had a big, old-fashioned radio at home that looked like the opening of a cave. I used to sit on the floor, almost inside the radio, and listen to the enchanting strains of "Pepsi-Cola hits the spot. . . ."

Not my friend Edna, however. While I huddled up to my

radio drinking in musical culture, Edna was home practicing scales or on her way downtown for another singing lesson. One day after school she asked me to go with her to the studio on West Seventy-third Street where she took lessons. I thought it might be fun, so I said, "All right, Edna, but I hope your teacher won't mind."

"Oh, Uncle Harry would love it. He might even ask you to sing for him—He always does."

"Oh, no, Edna, I can't sing like you."

"How do you know, smartie?"

With our books under our arms, we took the subway downtown and marched into Uncle Harry's studio at four o'clock. I remember there was an upright piano and some over-plushy furniture. On the piano I saw a picture of a girl in a man's costume. Later I learned it was Risë Stevens as Octavian in Strauss's *Der Rosenkavalier*.

Uncle Harry was a very jovial and energetic man, one of the thousands of "Uncle Harrys" floating around, a lovable fellow who made everybody feel at home the moment they entered his studio. Parado was his last name, though nobody ever used it.

"Another pupil?" he asked.

"No," said Edna, "just a friend from school who'd like to listen, Uncle Harry."

"Fine—let's give her something good to listen to, Edna."

Edna had a deep, beautiful voice, and I think she was destined to be a good singer, though it just didn't work out that way in her case. She was a quite stout little girl of ten, but sweet and pretty. Uncle Harry started her on a song, and when it was over, he turned to me.

"Do you sing at all?"

I said, "No, sir."

"Have you never studied singing? Call me Uncle Harry."

"No, Uncle Harry."

"How about trying to sing something for me—anything at all?"

Edna struck me as such a wonderful singer that I didn't dare even suggest I might want to sing a note—or could.

"But I don't know anything by heart," I pleaded.

"Oh, come on, you must know *something.*"

"There's nothing I really remember, sir—I mean Uncle Harry."

"Well, sing 'The Star-Spangled Banner.' You ought to know that all through."

So I sang "The Star-Spangled Banner" for Uncle Harry, and after the last note I was almost startled to hear him cry out, "Very good!" And he came and gave me a gentle pat on the back.

"Now, then," he said, "suppose you sing a few scales for me."

"Scales?" I said. "I don't know what they are."

"What? You mean to say you've never heard anybody sing scales?"

I shook my head. So Uncle Harry went to the piano and proceeded to show me what he wanted me to do. And for the first time in my life I sang scales, just a few of them. Then he went on with Edna's lesson, and when it was over, he asked me for my address. I gave it to him, and we left. When I got home I told my mother where I had been and what Uncle Harry had said.

"Could I go there like Edna and study singing, Mom? Could I?"

"Oh, I don't think so . . . but we'll see."

We waited a day or so. Whenever I had the chance, I kept pestering my mother to let me go and study with Uncle Harry. The more I thought about it, the more I liked the idea of going for a lesson, and maybe learning a few songs, with no idea, of course, that anything might come out of it. I began to think that it might be nice to sing at parties like Edna—or even at school.

Then we got a letter from Uncle Harry.

"Your daughter has real talent," he wrote. "She has the makings of a great voice. Will you please call me and arrange to come down to my studio. I'd like to talk to you about starting her on some lessons with me."

The very next night, after she returned from work, Mother took me down to West Seventy-third Street to Uncle Harry's studio.

"I'm positive I can do something with Roberta," he said to my mother. "In fact, I'll have her singing in no time at all. I'm working on something right now that ought to interest you."

And he told us about a children's radio program he used to have on WJZ several years before, a program of operatic arias, duets, trios, and choruses for which Milton Cross used to do the announcing.

"I'm hoping in the near future to get this program going again, and I think Roberta could fit very nicely into it. I've got lots of other kids working with me."

Mother said the idea sounded good to her.

"I'll also give Roberta private lessons—and I won't charge anything."

At that, Mother immediately began to protest.

"No, no, Mr. Parado, I couldn't think of it!"

So they argued back and forth, with neither of them yielding, and finally Uncle Harry gave a sigh of surrender and said, "Oh, all right, pay me a dollar for every lesson Roberta takes with me."

And that's how it began, at one dollar a lesson twice a week; Saturdays at one, when I had no school, and Wednesdays at seven-thirty, when I had school. Total weekly expenditures: two dollars. Mother always came along. Edna and her mother accompanied us on Wednesday nights, which were reserved for the group operatic work.

The first thing I want to say about Uncle Harry is that he never hurt my voice. As I look back on it, I suppose I have to admit that he didn't know too much about voice or singing, not in the best technical sense. I feel certain he was self-taught, and even his piano playing was slightly on the self-instructed side. I remember how he used to play with his eyes closed and how enthralled we were by what we thought was the greatest piano playing of our time—till one day I made a discovery. I noticed that when someone else would play the same song for me, it would always sound different. Sometimes I hardly recognized it as the same song. Uncle Harry loved to throw in all sorts of fancy embroidery. There was nothing systematic about him. I think he was a deeply artistic person, however— even without any real vocal or musical background.

The second thing he did for me—and this is really important —was to instill a love of opera in me that hadn't been there before. There was no opera at all in my background. I had never even heard an opera, let alone been to one, nor had my mother and father. We just weren't interested, I guess. Uncle Harry soon took care of that. With him, opera—especially Italian opera—was the beginning and end of all music; there was nothing else like it anywhere. It was a passion with him, his food and drink, the air he breathed, and a way of life. That's what he gave me, and it wasn't a small thing. And Uncle Harry wasn't even Italian! In spite of his name, he was Polish.

It wasn't very long before he had me singing Verdi and Puccini. At first we concentrated on scales. Even there he wasn't very methodical or demanding. I recall how excited I was whenever he had me do a double scale, that is a scale of two octaves, from middle C to high C. That would be the high

point of my lesson. I was still only ten when I began singing
grand opera in Uncle Harry's studio.

You'd never believe what we used to sing for him. "Miserere"
from *Il Trovatore* was one number. Another was the quartet
from *Rigoletto*, a third the duet from *Norma,* and a fourth the
trio from *Faust*.

Of course, Uncle Harry had no tenors. So pretty soon, to
round out the duets, and trios, and quartets, ten-year-old
Roberta Peterman became the star tenor of "The Harry Parado
Opera Company." I made my debut as tenor in the role of
Manrico in *Il Trovatore*. Later came the Duke in *Rigoletto*
and the title role of *Faust*. Since we were all expected to
double in brass—and it took a lot of juvenile brass to do it—
I was also the mezzo-soprano in Bellini's *Norma*. Some of these
ensembles we sang in Italian and some in English. I don't think
either language was recognizable to an outsider, the way we
mangled it.

At about the time of my twelfth birthday, Uncle Harry
began to ply me with solo asignments. My very first aria must
have been "Caro nome" from *Rigoletto*. I haven't the slightest
recollection how I did it, or, for that matter, why. I know it
was in Italian, but what Italian! Another was "Vissi d'arte"
from Puccini's *Tosca*. That passionate outburst I sang in
English: "Love and music . . . these have I lived for!" I returned to Italian, if you can call it that, for my first bout with
"Ah, fors' è lui" from *La Traviata*—a bout that I'm afraid Verdi
lost.

A fourth aria that Uncle Harry gave me to sing was "Robert,
toi que j'aime" from Meyerbeer's *Robert le Diable*. That one
I did in English, bent down on one knee, my hands clasped
together.

"Ah, Robert, Robert beloved!" I sang, in tones quavering
with adoration.

Uncle Harry had a way of fastening nicknames on his pupils

that stuck. "Comfy" was his pet name for one girl. Another girl was called "Feather," because she was so thin. A third was nicknamed "Cookie." One day he called me "Rosina," why, I never knew, because I never sang (until much later) Rosina's aria from *The Barber of Seville* for him. For some prophetic reason, Rosina it was and Rosina it remained.

It was in Uncle Harry's studio that I was first exposed to some of the great voices of the past. Listening to records became quite a ritual. Uncle Harry would bubble over with words of introduction, and presently the voice of Farrar, of Ponselle, of Galli-Curci, of Caruso, would be flooding the plushly upholstered studio.

At home, meanwhile, the musical atmosphere was changing fast. Singing commercials were a thing of the past, and the dial was always being turned, by mother, dad, or me, to wherever we could locate anything that sounded like an operatic aria. Then came our first piano. Uncle Harry was always telling me how important it was to have one. He never gave me any exercises or scales to do at home, but he did want me to work at the songs so that I would know them a little better the next time I came. So, after a few family conferences, in which the pros and cons were weighed (mostly in dollars and cents), we went out one Saturday afternoon and bought a piano. It was Uncle Harry who had spotted it for us—a second-hand baby grand which had seen and heard better days, but to me the most beautiful piano in the world.

The next thing you know I had another teacher. Her name was Miss Wagner. Very slowly, she started me off on scales, using one of the Diller-Quaile books. It wasn't too long before we were working on the Clementi sonatinas. At the piano I found my sense of the beauty and meaning of music growing every day. It was probably that secondhand baby grand, more than anything else, that first showed me what a discipline music was—and how much I wanted it. I went on to Mozart,

Beethoven, and Chopin with Miss Wagner, but by then I had
left Uncle Harry and moved on to another vocal studio.

It was shortly after my twelfth birthday that Mother began
to wonder what was going to happen next, if anything. I had
been with Uncle Harry for two years. Mother thought it time
to ask someone who really knew whether I had potentialities
that might grow into something worthwhile; in other words,
whether it would pay to go ahead—even at a dollar a lesson.

Enter Jan Peerce.

My grandfather, Leon Hirsch, at the time was manager of
the dining room at Grossinger's summer resort in the Catskills.
Mr. Peerce, the noted Metropolitan tenor, used to go there
for his vacations, and it was there that my grandfather sidled
up to him one day and began,

"I have a little granddaughter..."

Now Mr. Peerce had heard of little granddaughters from
numerous other grandparents. But he evidently liked my grandfather, so he said that he would like very much to hear me sing.
Well, this went on for some time, and the opportunity somehow
never seemed to come. It wasn't long before my grandfather's
death that he once more approached Mr. Peerce.

"If anything happens to me, Mr. Peerce," he said, "could
you at least let the girl's mother and father know if she's got
a voice."

Mr. Peerce gave his word, and when my grandfather told my
mother about it, she began calling him. But each time he
seemed to be busy. Even now Mr. Peerce says that every time
he picked up the phone it was Mrs. Peterman calling about
her daughter Roberta. Finally, he invited us to join him for
a cup of coffee one afternoon, after a rehearsal at the Metropolitan. Mother then asked him point-blank if he would please
listen to me sing.

"We will be guided by whatever you say, Mr. Peerce. We
want you to tell us whether Roberta should go on or just

forget about it and grow up and not think about singing any more."

"That's quite a responsibility," said Mr. Peerce. "I'll tell you what. Meet me next week at the same time in my accompanist's apartment. His name is Werner Bass, and he's on West Seventy-second Street."

The following week Mother and I went to Mr. Bass's apartment. While Mr. Peerce sat in a corner and listened, I sang, with Mr. Bass accompanying me. I think I did terribly. I couldn't help being nervous. I was so awed by Jan Peerce— the fact that he had actually gone out of his way to hear me sing.

I had the gall to sing "Ah, fors' è lui" from *Traviata* and "Vissi d'arte" from *Tosca*—a twelve-year-old child trying to impress a leading Metropolitan tenor! I think he was quite surprised, but all he said was, "It sounds pretty good."

Mother and I didn't know what to think. Without saying a word, we waited as Mr. Peerce stroked his chin thoughtfully.

"I tell you what," he said. "Let's all go down to a friend of mine. I want him to hear you sing."

So we went down to a lower floor of the same apartment house. Mr. Peerce's friend was none other than Paul Althouse, the great American tenor. After the introductions, I felt more awed than ever in the presence of these two experts. When Mr. Althouse asked me to sing, I repeated the aria from *Traviata*.

"Very, very good," he said, coming up to me. I saw him examining me very oddly.

"You have a very stout neck," he said. "Wonderful!"

I think he saw from the look on my face that I wanted to ask him what was wonderful about it but didn't dare.

"All the very greatest singers have stout necks," he remarked matter-of-factly, and before I could stutter anything like a reply, he said, "Come with me."

Mr. Althouse took me into another room, where he had photographs of a great number of singers, among them Luisa Tetrazzini.

"Look at their necks," he said. "Now do you see what I mean? I think it's extraordinary that you should have such a neck—extraordinary."

Stout neck or not, when it came to discuss chances of studying with him, he shook his head.

"I don't accept children or beginners. I'm sorry. But if you wait a while, till you grow up a bit, I would be happy to give you some lessons."

That was that. Mother, Mr. Peerce, and I thanked Mr. Althouse for his courtesy and walked back upstairs to Mr. Bass's apartment, where we discussed our problem a little further.

"My advice is to go on studying," said Mr. Peerce. "But try not to think that something has to come out of it—that you're a child prodigy, or anything like that. Study anyway."

I wasn't too sure I liked leaving things there.

"Mr. Peerce," I said, "I want to study some songs, popular and semipopular, so that maybe I can do a little singing somewhere."

Mother joined in. "Isn't there somebody you could suggest who wouldn't mind taking a child?"

"All right," said Mr. Peerce, slapping his thigh, "if it's popular songs you want, let's try Matty Levine."

Matty Levine turned out to be a good coach for learning the hit show tunes of the day, as well as the middle repertory that includes selections from the better-type operettas. I remember he taught me to do "Out of My Dreams" in the style of the day. I stayed only six months with Mr. Levine. At the end of that time I felt he wasn't quite what I wanted and needed. He was doing wonders for others, but I guess we just didn't hit it off too brilliantly as teacher and pupil. However, during those six months I appeared on a few "Kiddie Shows," and it was Mr. Levine who helped me work out the songs I sang. I auditioned for the Horn and Hardart and Nick Kenny shows. I sang "One Kiss" on one of Mr. Kenny's programs. When I had finished and while we were still on the air, he said to me, "Solle sein mit Glick from Uncle Nick."

I sang for Nick Kenny twice again after that, and I wonder if he knows that I'm the little girl who sang for him ten years before. Probably he doesn't, because then I went under my real name of Roberta Peterman. If he ever sees this, I want him to know I always treasured that good-luck send-off "from Uncle Nick."

I also made my first recording at that time, strictly unofficially. I sang Juliet's waltz from Gounod's *Roméo et Juliette*. Matty Levine played the piano for me. Everything went fine, till the last cadenza. I forgot completely how it went! I didn't stop, however. Fresh kid that I was, I made up my own cadenza. What I sang I don't recall, and how I did it I don't know, but I do know this: I finished right on pitch, and I took the high notes just as I was supposed to. My ad-libbing fitted in perfectly with the upper notes. When I finished with the top tone just where Gounod put it, everybody was surprised—most of all me.

During all that time I hadn't gone above high C. That was the highest I had ever *thought* about. In no song or aria that I had sung had I attempted anything higher. Very high arias like *Caro Nome* were transposed down. The fact is I didn't think much of the notes, high or low. What I loved to sing were the words. I have always been drawn to the meaning of words, so I had been concentrating on that. I never knew what I was doing vocally, or why. I knew the pitch—that was never hard for me. It seemed to come like second nature. And the rhythm also came easily, almost instinctively. But I never really knew what to do with my voice. No one had ever men-

tioned breathing, or sustaining a note, or quality. That was
still a foreign language to me. I just knew I loved the words,
and that's what I sang. . . .

When my six months with Matty Levine were over, Mother
and I called up Mr. Peerce to ask for another consultation.
A meeting was again arranged in a restaurant after a rehearsal
at the Met. About that time we were all reading about Patrice
Munsel, then a seventeen-year-old girl who had just won the
Metropolitan Auditions of the Air. While we were having our
second cup of coffee with Mr. Peerce, we asked him about
Patrice Munsel, what he thought about her, who her teacher
was, whether he thought her teacher would be the right person
to train me.

"Oh, yes, I know Bill Herman," said Mr. Peerce. "Why don't
you call him up and say I advised you to go to him for an
audition. It can never hurt."

Later that afternoon, Mother called up Mr. Herman, who
said he would be happy to hear anyone recommended by Jan
Peerce, and could we come up to his studio that Saturday at
twelve noon? Mother paused to consult me. I hesitated a moment, then said Yes.

The reason I hesitated was that at ten thirty that same
Saturday morning I was to sing on Hearn's "Kiddie Show."
But I felt an audition with Patrice Munsel's teacher wasn't
anything to trifle with. That Saturday I went on the air and
sang one of Deanna Durbin's hit songs, "A Heart That's Free."
Deanna was my movie idol at that time—I still had no opera
idol—and I had gotten the song from an album of hers. After
I sang it, the emcee suddenly remarked, "Those are cute bangs
you have."

"Thank you," said I.

"What type voice do you have?"

Without a moment's hesitation, I announced solemnly: "I
am a coloratura."

Where I got the word I don't know. I knew I had a voice, but that's all. Nobody had ever bothered to put a label on it. All of this was strictly impromptu, while we were still on the air.

"Do you think your voice will ever change?"

"It might," I said, "but I hope it doesn't."

And then, in a falsetto, high-pitched voice, imitating me, he said:

"I'm a coloratura too, and I hope my voice doesn't change either."

Mother and I were feeling quite good when we left Loew's State Building at Broadway and Forty-fifth Street and headed for the nearest uptown subway entrance. Mr. Herman's studio was then located on Seventy-ninth Street and Riverside Drive. It was exactly twelve o'clock when the door opened. I came in carrying my little briefcase. We were asked to wait a few minutes, while Mr. Herman finished a lesson in the studio. When it was over, I went in, and a sturdy, square-shouldered man of alert and sensitive features greeted me cordially.

"How old are you?" was his very first question.

"Thirteen, sir," I said, still standing.

"Please sit down, little girl, and relax," he said. "There's nothing to be nervous about."

I did as he told me. We talked for a while, and I could see he was trying to draw me out. He wanted to know what I had already done, what subjects I liked in school, where I had studied singing. I answered as best I could.

"What sort of music do you like?"

"Songs," I said.

"How about opera?"

"I don't know too much about opera," I said.

"Tell me, what songs do you know?"

"Oh," I said, " 'One Kiss' and 'A Heart That's Free.' I also know 'I Passed by Your Window.' "

"That's quite a romantic repertory," he said. "What would you like to sing for me today?"

"*La Traviata*," I said.

"Hm," commented Mr. Herman, lifting his eyebrows and saying nothing more.

He called in his accompanist and asked him to do the aria, "*Ah, fors' è lui*" with me. Then he took a seat near Mother at the other end of the large studio. Halfway through the aria, I saw him beckon to me to stop. He came up to me.

"What do you think you're doing?" he asked.

"*La Traviata*," I answered innocently.

"Have you done this very often?"

I said, "No—only at my other teacher's studio."

"He permitted this?"

Unperturbed, I said: "Yes, sir."

"All right, let me hear the rest of it."

With that he returned to his place at the other end of the room, and I finished the aria.

"Are you aware," he said, "that you were waving your arms around like mad ..."

Silence.

"... that you had no real support under those tones?"

I nodded agreement, though I hadn't the faintest idea what he meant.

"However"—he drawled out the word—"however, I think you have the beginning of a very great talent. You have the feeling for the music, and what's more remarkable, for the mood of the words ..."

Another pause.

"... though I'm positive you don't know what they mean."

I thanked Mr. Herman demurely.

"Now listen carefully," he said. "I want you to take two weeks off from singing. No lessons with anybody. Don't think about singing at all. Understand?"

"Yes, Mr. Herman."

"I will call up Mr. Peerce," he went on, "and tell him that I have accepted you as my pupil. Now go home and relax—and come back in two weeks."

This is what I wrote down in my diary that Saturday night, January 15, 1944:

> Dear Diary: Today was very eventful. I got up early and sang on the Hearn's Show. After that we went to Patrice Munsel's teacher. I sang an aria from *La Traviata*. He said I squeaked each note, but that I have a beautiful voice. Also, that the song I sang was too difficult for me. But, dear diary, I don't need the Kiddie Shows any more. I want to study, and in a few years I'd like to sing at the Metropolitan. I know I have to study hard, and I resolve that I will. Good night.
>
> ROBERTA PETERMAN

2

"I Failed, Mr. Herman"

Age: 14

FOR the next two weeks I did what Mr. Herman had advised me to do: nothing.

That is, nothing except my daily routine of family, school, homework, and reading. No music. No singing. The two weeks were up on February 1, and I went for my first lesson with the teacher of Patrice Munsel.

I shall never forget that day. Mr. Herman just talked to—and at—me. He had a little chart showing what the throat looked like inside. I was interested for more reasons than one. About that time I was having a lot of trouble with my thyroid. I was always coming down with colds, and Mother was taking me from one doctor to another.

"We're going to work on breath control, Roberta," Mr. Herman announced.

"Yes, Mr. Herman."

"Breath support," he continued, "that and keeping the chest inflated at all times are the whole basis of good singing. Will you repeat that?"

I did.

"The Italians say, *'Chi non appoggia non canta.'* Have you any idea what that means?"

"No, Mr. Herman."

"It means, 'Who doesn't support, doesn't sing.' Will you remember that?"

"Yes, Mr. Herman. 'Who doesn't support, doesn't sing.'"

There was no danger of my forgetting it. That statement became a theme song of the lessons that followed—SUPPORT, SUPPORT, SUPPORT.

"Once you grasp that," said Mr. Herman, "you'll never be out of breath at the end of a musical phrase."

Then he looked stern.

"And furthermore, there's no need for waving your arms around as if you were signaling an approaching train."

I must have looked a little abashed.

"But that's to be expected," he said. "We'll soon have to consider getting you somebody to teach you dramatics and Italian. Would you like that?"

"Oh, I'd love it, Mr. Herman!"

It won't do you any harm to know what you're singing," he said. "After all, the composer had to know what the words were all about before he could think of the right music for them. The words, Roberta, the words!"

"Yes, Mr. Herman."

"You've heard of the proverb, I suppose, about a healthy mind in a healthy body?"

"I have, Mr. Herman, and I believe it."

"You do? That's fine. Now we will go one step farther and make it a healthy voice in a healthy body. Exercise is very important."

He suggested that I go to a gymnasium once or twice a week.

"It is a very hard road, Roberta," said Mr. Herman, "and

a long and lonely road. It isn't just the singing. It's the languages, too—the Italian and the French and the German. It's the dramatics. All of these things go into the making of a singer. It's going to be study, study, study. All set?"

"All set, Mr. Herman."

That was all. No singing, no scales; only talk. The lesson had lasted a half hour. There were to be two a week, on Tuesday and Thursday.

At my second lesson we began to work on scales—small scales. Mr. Herman didn't let me go up too high, not at first.

"I want to see how the voice sounds in the middle range," he said, "and how flexible it is."

Before I began with Mr. Herman, I had never gone above a high C. After the second or third lesson, we started to climb up beyond the middle range to the higher notes. We did a great number of arpeggios up to C, D, and E. Mr. Herman was quite pleased with my trill—that is, after I had mastered it.

The trill needed work, hard work, of course. The voice was agile enough at first, but it required drilling. Gradually I got the trick of it and my voice was exactly the way he wanted it, which was to make the two notes of the trill heard with equal clearness.

After my fifth lesson I was going up to A and B-flat above high C in scalework.

It was at my fourth or fifth lesson that he again brought up the subject of coaching.

"I have a lady in mind for you for dramatic study," he said. "Her name is Stabile, a very charming and scholarly Italian lady. She will teach you Italian too. But she's ill now, and we'll have to wait a week or two."

I told Mr. Herman I was happy at the thought of studying with her. I had complete confidence in everything he advised me to do.

The first exercise book Mr. Herman gave me was García's

Vocal Method. I have always treasured this excellent manual, and I hope to use it for the rest of my life as a singer.

The book is perfect for the study of scales in all their gradations. It also explains in great detail and clarity things like the formation of registers, sustained sounds, swelled sounds, *canto vellutato. . . .*

García's *Vocal Method* first made me aware that there are many kinds of singing. If I did a simple song, the simplicity of the song was the most attractive part of it. When it was a song that required a lot of agility, the technique became the most appealing feature. These were vividly explained in the text.

I began to see what *legato* meant, and *marcato.* The book was full of little explanations, diagrams, with music. Mr. Herman and I would pore over it together, discuss it till everything was clear.

Then he would call in the accompanist, who would play the scales for us. And I would go through them very slowly, very carefully.

There would be the sustained notes, for instance, taken slowly to keep the voice even and equal and to keep out any trace of a tremolo. We were working for firmness and purity of tone. The sustained sounds, Mr. Herman said, were the most difficult to do right.

I never differed with Mr. Herman, of course, but I'd ask lots and lots of questions.

"Why are the sustained sounds the most difficult?"

"Because," said Mr. Herman, "it is so hard to hold this unchanging firmness. And that's what the sustained notes do."

"How do they affect the breathing?" I wanted to know.

"They help the breath support," he said. "If you know you have to hold a tone for four or five bars, you have to know how to distribute the breath so as to give enough and yet not be completely out of breath at the end of the note."

Mr. Herman always believed in showing me these vocal processes in diagrams and illustrations.

"I've always felt, Roberta," he said, "that it helps a singer to have an idea of what the machinery of singing looks like. These sustained and swelled sounds. What makes them that way? There's always something happening inside your throat. And if there's something happening, it can be shown on a chart."

I found it all fascinating—the theory and the practice both. I remember how excited I was working on the "swelled" sound. I'd start very slow, swelling the note to a crescendo, and returning to a decrescendo. Then the other way, starting the note full, then a decrescendo, and finally a crescendo—all on one note.

That we did for "proportioning" the breath.

"You have a weak chest, Roberta," Mr. Herman startled me by saying one day. "I don't mean you have anything to be alarmed about. But you'll have to build it up to help develop your breath support."

That's where the gymnasium came in.

Back to García. With Mr. Herman's help, I kept finding ever new things in his *Vocal Methods*. It was like a journey of discovery for me. All those tricky little ways of embellishing the main note, either before or after it.

I learned that the things I was doing were called *accacciatura, mordenti, gruppetti*. I loved the very sound of those words. And what they stood for too.

And what they stood for was:

COLORATURA!

I took to it like a duck takes to water. I had used the word in a broadcast without the slightest notion what it meant. Now I knew it was meant for me—or I for it. Coloratura.

Mr. Herman saw at once how joyously I responded to this type of work, how after I had a lesson, I would always come back the next time with all or most of what he had told me fully assimilated. I seemed to be always asking for more to do, to learn, to sing.

Then came my first songs. How proud I was the day Mr. Herman gave me a list of the songs he wanted me to buy! And what a serious little miss went into the music store to ask for them. Among the very first were: "Bonnie Sweet Bessie," "The Wren," "The Gypsy and the Bird," "I'd Be a Butterfly."

Each had a quality of its own. "Bonnie Sweet Bessie," charming, plaintive, simple in phrasing and melody, is still in my concert repertory. It is simple, but deep in inner feeling and emotion. I loved it too for its "swelled" sounds and sustained singing.

"The Wren" and "The Gypsy and the Bird" called for more flexibility. They were cute and sweet, tricky and on the surface. This was what the books and Mr. Herman called *canto d'agilità*—agile singing.

"I'd Be a Butterfly" was just a sprightly little English song— whimsical, a plaything for the voice.

I think Mr. Herman gave me the songs to make me feel he had confidence in me. You see, for weeks all I did was scales. It was fun mastering the tricks, but I began to feel I wanted to sink my teeth into a real melody. He saw that, I think.

It was only many years later that he told me what he had in mind when he first heard me sing "Bonnie Sweet Bessie" for him.

"I saw the little girl standing there," he said, "pouring her little heart right out. I knew then I had been right about you. I said to myself, 'This is destined to be great.'"

That song is still one of my favorites—like a luck charm, perhaps. It is the simplest of songs, a little Scottish melody. It lies well in my voice, although at the very beginning my middle voice wasn't quite what it should have been.

That part of my voice was a little "covered." The tone wasn't as clear in the middle as it was in the high register. It was strictly a technical thing. I worked very hard to remove that "veil" and make my voice free all through its range.

And yet that veiling in the voice gave the song as I did it a sad and mystical quality, and the song *is* sad. There was nothing brittle about the tone at the end, one of the high notes. I was able to spin the tone, an A-natural, as a *messa di voce*. I went from diminuendo to crescendo and back to diminuendo again, all on the one A-natural. Mr. Herman was pleased with me, and I suppose I was too.

"You showed a true instinct for the words and the music as the story unfolded," he said to me.

I regarded that as quite a compliment.

Then came one of the worst jolts to my pride that I have ever experienced. It was now late in spring and we were approaching the end of my term at school. I thought it would be nice to try out for admission to the High School of Music and Art. It is one of the finest secondary schools in New York, and almost every youngster interested in the arts at some time or other toys with the hope of being accepted there. Admission is solely on the basis of written and oral examination. Merit alone—no pressure, no favoritism.

My music teacher, Mrs. Secor, arranged my application after I told her I wanted to try out for the school. A date was set for me to go for an examination. I was required to sing something and I chose "I'd Be a Butterfly" and "Bonnie Sweet Bessie." As my piano piece I played Mozart's first *Sonata in C*. There was also an ear test—tones, tone quality, relative pitch— and a written musical test: "What does a half note look like?" and that sort of thing.

Well, I took the test. I felt so confident that honestly I thought I was running away with it. Both my music teachers at school, Mrs. Secor and Mrs. O'Mara, were positive I would get in. I must admit I was a little nervous. I must have muffed some of the questions, either in the written or the oral part of the examination. I wasn't in the very best voice. Yet I was sure they liked my singing and I never had a moment's doubt they would take me.

I had gone into the examination with four other girls from my school, P.S. 117, Wade Junior High. All four of my companions were positive I would make it, and they were just as positive that they wouldn't. Well, we waited for the results. The news came about two weeks later.

I was called out of the classroom by my music teacher, Mrs. Secor. Very gently and with the utmost friendliness, she took me into one of the teachers' restrooms. And she told me.

"They didn't take you, Roberta."

That was all.

I was crushed. I suddenly felt weak and sick. I couldn't say a word. Then I burst out crying bitterly. Mrs. Secor tried to console me. She tried to minimize the blow. She soothed my wounded pride. But she saw it would be cruel to expect me to continue school that day.

"I think you'd better go home, Roberta," she said. "Sometimes these things are for the best. Watch and see."

I took hold of myself when she left me. I went into the washroom, wiped my eyes, and tried to calm down. I had to steel myself to tell Bill Herman. It must have been 11:30 A.M. I was surprised at how this thing had shocked and stunned me. I had immediately lost all confidence. How could I fail, I asked myself, when everybody, including myself, was so sure I'd pass? How could I face anyone now? Two of the others, I found out soon enough, had made it, and that, being only human, didn't make it any more agreeable for me. One of the girls, to make matters worse, was a sort of rival, a friendly and amiable rival. She was mainly a piano student, though she also sang. Her name was Hannah Brimat. Well, Hannah got in, and I didn't. What a blow to my young ego! I just couldn't face all those kids that day, Hannah included. They had all been expecting such big things of me, studying with a big voice teacher and all that, and here I was, my first real test, and I had flunked out. I couldn't even pass the simplest test in music. I never felt smaller or more humiliated in my life.

So I went straight home and called up Mr. Herman. Without saying why, I asked him if I could come down to see him. I remember it was a mild, sunny day. Mr. Herman had a small balcony outside his apartment on Riverside Drive. The balcony window was open when I arrived and he took me outside. For a moment we both stood there in silence looking down at the Hudson River.

"I failed, Mr. Herman."

To my great surprise, he took it very calmly, as if somehow he already knew or perhaps even wanted it that way.

"Oh, don't take this seriously. It doesn't mean a thing.... First of all, I've got other plans for you."

I looked up at him expectantly.

"...and second of all, did you know that Giuseppe Verdi was not accepted when he applied for admission at one of the music schools?"

This made me laugh. I know he threw that in to make light of my little tragedy. I must have looked very solemn to him. I can just see myself, a rueful little girl only a few hours earlier absolutely sure of herself, and now completely deflated. Well, with a little coddling and a little comedy, I allowed myself to be convinced.

Mr. Herman proceeded to show me why it wasn't the most important thing in the world. That my actual singing and my integrity must help me through moments like that. That I must have a philosophy. That this was not the whole world, and that it hadn't come to an end yet.

"The most important thing, Roberta, is your singing," he said. "If that's what you really want and love and need, you must stick to it. Tests are not important."

"Mr. Herman," I cried, "my singing means everything to me, more than everything else, except my father and mother."

"That's fine!" he said. "Now let's go in and have a lesson."

That balcony scene has stayed vividly in my memory. A gentle breeze blew up from the Hudson. The river glistened there below in the sun, and two or three large boats were coming downstream. In the park, far down below us, children were running and shouting and laughing. I suddenly felt sure that Mr. Herman was right. I went into the studio with him and started to sing, and the more I sang the more I forgot about the test I had failed. In fact, I forgot all about everything except what a joy it was to be alive on a spring day like this—and to sing! That is what counted.

3

"It Means a Lot of Sacrifice..."

Age: 14

OUT on the balcony that day, Mr. Herman had said he had "other plans" for me.

I didn't find out what they were till I finished my term at school. Meanwhile, I worked on my singing and music and languages through the summer of 1944. It was September and I was about to enroll for my next grade in Junior High, when Mr. Herman called and asked the three of us—Mother, Father, and me—to come down to his studio to discuss something with him. We went down the following evening, after Dad and Mother had finished work. Mr. Herman came right to the point.

"I think that Roberta has the makings of a real talent. The possibilities of a great career are all there. Now, the only way we can help this talent is to give it all the leeway we can, the spaciousness to go ahead. Nothing must stand in its way."

I could see that Father and Mother were deeply impressed, but also a little puzzled. I know I was. It all sounded as if some grave and momentous decision would have to be made.

"Naturally, we would never allow anything to stand in Roberta's way," said my father.

"There must be no obstacles of any kind," Mr. Herman went on.

"I'm sure we've done everything you asked us to do, Mr. Herman," said Mother.

"You've both been extremely cooperative," said Mr. Herman, "and extremely trustful. Now I ask you to go one step farther. Have I your full confidence in whatever I advise?"

"You know you have, Mr. Herman."

"Well, then, I think Roberta should be taken out of public school," he said. "Are you prepared to place all responsibility in me?"

Mother and Dad looked at one another for a moment and then at me. We were all at a loss.

"We do," said Dad, "but could you explain why such a drastic step is necessary now?"

"We are going on the assumption that we have something very worthwhile here," said Mr. Herman. "Something that a daily routine at school might interfere with at this point.

"Attending class from nine to three every weekday will take Roberta away from her vocal studies. She must begin working now in preparation for a serious career as a singer. That will take all her time."

Dad still had some doubts. I could see that, like Mother and me, he was awed by Mr. Herman's picture of my future. But it was quite a step, after all.

"What about a diploma?" he said. "Isn't it needed, and where would Roberta ever get it if we took her out of school?"

Mr. Herman turned to me.

"What about it, Roberta? Do you think you can manage without a diploma?"

"I think I'd like one, Mr. Herman," I said.

"Well, you can always go back when you want to—after achieving your goal," he said.

I was really very excited about leaving school, especially after my failure to be admitted at the High School of Music and Art. I wanted so much to give all my time to singing.

Mr. Herman must have been studying the expression on my face.

"Do you like the idea, Roberta?"

"Oh, I love it, Mr. Herman!" I shouted.

"We have so much confidence in you," said Dad. "If it's what Roberta wants, then it's what we want, too."

"Good!" said Mr. Herman. "Then we'll stop worrying about diplomas. I must be given a free hand in whatever concerns her education. I want to be sure that whatever I advise Roberta to do, she will do."

"I think you can count on her and on us, Mr. Herman," said Mother.

"You see," said Mr. Herman, "if you give a person the responsibility, you must give him the authority, too. And now a special word for you, Roberta."

I had rarely seen Mr. Herman look so grave as at that moment.

"It means a lot of sacrifice, young lady. You won't be an average girl in the sense that you won't have what people regard as a normal life. You can't be that type of girl any more.

"There will be little room for the usual kind of play. You won't be able to go to school dances and participate in the normal activities of a girl your age."

Mr. Herman paused. Mother and Dad were looking at me in a strange way, almost as if they wanted to speak up and call the whole thing off. I could see it was a dreadful moment of decision for the three of us.

"You've got to think of all that, Roberta," Mr. Herman went on, "and now is the last time to do it."

I could feel my heart pounding. I knew this was a turning point in my life, that I would never be able to go back. I also knew, from the expressions on their faces, that Mother and Dad were a little alarmed, but that they were leaving it up to me.

"Do you still think you want to?" asked Mr. Herman.

In a flash I went over all the things he said I would have to do without, and suddenly they didn't seem to matter very much. I knew the other was the life I wanted and I didn't want any of them to have any doubt about it. It was going to be *my* decision, not his nor Mother's nor Dad's.

"I do, I do, Mr. Herman!" I cried out. "I don't care about the dancing and the games. I don't care about parties and going to the movies and vacations. I want above everything else in the world to become a singer, and a good one, Mr. Herman, and I promise to be guided by you at all times."

"*Brava!*" said Mr. Herman, and turning to my parents, he asked, "And how about you?"

"If that is what Roberta wants more than anything else, we want it, too," said my mother. "We just don't want to feel she is cheating herself of a normal life."

"Our only wish is to see her happy," said Dad. "We will do everything to help."

"And now for some practical matters," said Mr. Herman. "I know you're not wealthy, and I propose to help as much as I can."

Mr. Herman asked my parents what their financial status was and how much they thought they could contribute toward the cost of my studies.

"I will make it a partial scholarship," he explained. "Can you afford to pay me eighty dollars a month for the lessons I give Roberta?"

"That is very generous, Mr. Herman," said Dad.

"Well, if you can pay that, I'll take care of some of the other things," said Mr. Herman. "I will pay for the language lessons, the dramatic coaching, and whatever else is required beyond the vocal training she will get from me."

Mother and Dad couldn't thank him enough. Yet, I don't think they were surprised at Mr. Herman's generous proposal. They knew how much he was interested in me and how confidently he believed in my future.

They had seen me come home from each lesson as if from a great new adventure. They had seen this growing excitement in me, this determination to go ahead in this business of singing. They had seen a glow on my face that had never been there before. So, of course, they were happy to make the arrangement with Bill Herman.

I'm sure they knew there would be days of regret, days when they would wonder whether after all I shouldn't have remained in school and enjoyed the games and the parties and the dances like all the other children my age.

I think what made the decision easy for the three of us, apart from Mr. Herman's interest and enthusiasm, was that we were secure in each other's love. We were all so happy together at home. They made life easy and smooth for me, and rich in all the warmth and attention and protection that a young girl needs.

I couldn't have said Yes to Mr. Herman if it hadn't been for that. I could never have done it alone—the work, work, work, and no play in the six long years that followed, without the love and gentleness of these two sweet people. They were my only real companions, they and Bill Herman; and they sufficed.

There was still the problem of telling the principal of my school. Would he consent? After all, this was an unusual step, and a responsible one for everyone concerned, including the school authorities. I know I worried quite a bit about that trip to the office of the principal, Mr. Schoenberg. Mr. Herman had told me what to say, but I was a little nervous.

As I glibly outlined the plan to Mr. Schoenberg, I remember I kept saying to myself, "He's going to say No; he's not going to believe me."

"It's a music school, you say, Roberta?" he asked.

"Yes, Mr. Schoenberg."

"Its name?"

I paused to gulp.

"The William Herman School of Singing."

"Mmm; sound's impressive," he said. "A private school, in other words."

"Yes, Mr. Schoenberg, and it will include languages and coaching and literature and lots and lots of music," I said.

"Well, I'm all for it—if you think it's right, and you do, don't you?"

"Oh, yes, Mr. Schoenberg, though I know I'll miss all my friends and teachers here. You've all been too wonderful to me."

"You've got to think of yourself only, and I'm persuaded this is absolutely the right course for you. I have great faith in you. We're going to make it very easy for you."

So I suppose he made some inquiries, got out my records, and discussed the matter with other members of the staff. He then gave his formal consent to my being taken out of school. I went to see each of my teachers to say good-bye. They were all happy for me, because they had known for so long that this was the direction I had always wanted to take. I was a little sad leaving them; they had all given me such encouragement, especially Mrs. Secor.

Apart from my father and mother, Bill Herman long meant more to me than any other person in my life. You would expect this devotion and attention from a parent. I was not attached to Bill Herman in any other way but as a pupil. Yet, how unselfish he was! Because of him and my parents, I never really missed anything in my long years of study.

Many people know how hard I've worked, and in the ordinary sense I was cheated of play and all the things that go with girlhood. There wasn't any room for the fun that goes with school and dates and parties. Maybe I did miss a little of that. But, and this is the truth, I never felt it, and that I owe to Bill Herman as much as to my parents.

He was a young man in spirit, in his philosophy. He had an optimistic outlook and loved life. There were no prejudices of any kind in him. Through him and his philosophy I was able to enjoy life and study all the time and never feel that I was being robbed of childhood.

We'd go for walks on Sundays; we'd listen to records together when my lesson was over.

I'd browse about his library, and he would urge me to take books home with me, if I expressed an interest in them. I couldn't count the times I took the subway back to the Bronx with an open book in my hands—and the times I missed my station.

All of that was more precious than I can say. Was it sacrifice? Not in the least, and I'm sure Mother and Father never doubted for long that we had made the right decision.

I remarked before that when Mr. Herman proposed taking me out of school, I brought up the question of a diploma. I kind of liked the idea of getting one. Who doesn't? Every school child looks forward to it as a great milestone in his or her life. There had to be some sacrifice in what I was doing, and that was part of the bargain. So I didn't let it bother me for long.

Well, just about the time of our great decision, Mr. Herman sprang another surprise on me. My first opera role! Up to then we had worked on exercises, songs, a few arias; but no full-length role. I was so thrilled the day he gave me the score, a beautiful old Italian edition. I took it tenderly in my hands and read, *"Lucia di Lammermoor."* I was thrilled beyond words.

"We're going to work on the whole role, Roberta," he said. "The score is a gift from me to you, and it is a token of the faith I have in you and of my pleasure in the way you have been responding to my lessons."

"Oh, Mr. Herman," I cried, overcome with joy and gratitude, "I hope I prove worthy of your faith. I'll try never to disappoint you, never, never!"

"You won't," he said. "You may read the inscription on your way home. Meanwhile, let's see what we already know about Donizetti and this opera of his, and who sang it, and just how we're going to prepare you to become one of the great Lucias."

The moment I left Mr. Herman and was out in the street on my way to the subway, I opened the score and read:

"To Roberta, my very dear pupil, with all my love—her first opera score."

It was signed "Maestro." The date under the inscription was September 16, 1944. I hugged the score to me and made a silent vow that I would never let this wonderful man down. I would work till I became everything he wanted me to be.

That night it was impossible for me to fall asleep. I couldn't tear myself away from the score. It gave me the strangest feeling: that I was already an opera singer; that it was now only a question of time.

Lucia di Lammermoor! That magic title has a very special ring to my ears. It was not only my first opera score and my first opera role. Mr. Herman has since told me something more.

It was this same role that ultimately convinced him I was ready for the Metropolitan.

That was my diploma.

4

"Feeling, Feeling, Roberta!"

Age: 14 to 19

ANTONIETTA STABILE was the name of the fine Italian lady to whom Mr. Herman sent me for my Italian lessons and dramatic coaching. He knew her as a good scholar and as a diseuse who had often appeared on the broadcasts of an Italian station that he once managed. Mme. Stabile used to read the love poems of Ada Negri to her Italo-American listeners, and also little bits of plays by Pirandello. She was known for her beautiful pronunciation and expressive delivery.

It was Mme. Stabile that Mr. Herman recommended to all his pupils for good Italian diction and literature. There is no way of conveying how much I owe to her.

Almost from the day we met, we spoke Italian. That was her theory. Begin as soon as possible. Get the language in both your ears and your eyes. Live as much as you can with the sound of it. There would be the merest fragments of grammar, and then we would talk, as far as my vocabulary would carry me—and even farther. That would be the work of one lesson.

Our next meeting would be devoted to *scena*: a complete
scene from a libretto. First, we would go over the translation.
She would ask me to read all the parts at home. Anything
I didn't understand I would write down in a notebook. Poetic
expressions, strange idioms, that sort of thing.

After we had gone over every word and phrase, Mme.
Stabile would play records of that scene by the great singers.
While the records played, I was expected to act out the char-
acter.

I never *sang* the lines for her; I only *spoke* them. That way
I wasn't obliged to use up my voice. I learned character and
action and plot and language, and I got a feeling for the
orchestral accompaniment—all without singing a single note.

Mme. Stabile would explain the character.

"This Lucia," I remember her saying, "is a northern woman;
remember that. She hasn't the southern gestures or the southern
walk."

And she would show me what she meant. She would go into
detail about the feelings of the character, the nature of the
conflict, how the fact that Lucia came from one part of Europe
rather than another affected her whole outlook on life and love.

"She was Scottish, this Lucy of Lammermoor, not Italian,
Roberta," she said. "The attitude of such a woman to her lover
would be very different from that of an Italian woman."

I took her word for it. After all, I was fourteen years old
and I had never been out on a date.

Mme. Stabile would paint in the period for me, the nature
of the drama against the historic background of feuds and
rivalries. She would act out the scenes with me. I would be
Lucy and she Alice. Mme. Stabile knew the whole libretto by
heart.

"Feeling, feeling, Roberta!" she would say. "Put feeling into
every word, every line, every note! Think of what that poor
girl is enduring!"

And only when she felt I had begun to make Lucia's feelings my own, when the character had become part of me, would she put the records on and have me act out the *scena* against the music.

I have a picture of her sitting there very quietly, watching every gesture of mine, and making notes on a little pad. I would try to let my feelings guide me.

"Don't imitate me," she would say over and over again. "Each gesture must come naturally to you, and it will if you feel the role."

When it was over she would read her notes to me: where I had felt it, where I had not; where I was sincere, where I was parroting her; where I was within the period of the opera, where I wasn't.

The stress was always on relaxation. To achieve this she used a principle she called *plastico del corpo*—the plasticity of the body. Every gesture had to look easy and natural.

"So natural," she would say, "that a person watching you would not think of it as a gesture at all, but as a revelation of feeling and character. Gestures, Roberta, are words that we cannot speak."

When we tackled the "Mad Scene" from *Lucia,* she would ask me:

"Where would you drop the knife? . . . Would Lucia be startled? . . . Would she just not be aware of it? . . . When she sees all the friendly faces, would her reflex be to relax, so that the knife would just naturally drop from her hand? . . ."

We would discuss these things. To make me see Lucia from another angle, she would even let me play the part of her lover Edgardo. She would take the role of Lucia. She played Figaro to my Rosina, and again she would reverse the roles, and I would do Figaro (a fourteen-year-old female Figaro!).

"The more roles you know of the same opera," she said,

"the more you will know the opera, its mood, its accent, its direction. And the better you will know your own role."

Once she made me do the role of the Duke in *Rigoletto.*

"It will help you to understand Gilda better," she said.

Sometimes it was hard for her to tell me things that were vital to the opera, as in the relation between Gilda and the Duke. She would explain about the period of *Rigoletto,* the customs and morals, and so on, how it was possible for such a man to behave so shamefully.

There was always this emphasis on the mood of the epoch; what the people thought and felt, the convention behind their behavior.

"It is just as important to know what is in the mind of your character," she said, "as it is to be able to sing what must come from her throat."

Then there would be whole sessions on the movements of the body. She would show me how to move my hands on the stage. To develop a graceful gesture she would give me the exercise of bringing my hand up and holding the fingers as if water were being cupped in them.

There was an exercise for the eyes, without a single movement of the face. There was a way of moving the wrist to relax it, and then moving it fast, so that the whole hand would relax. And what walking I did in that little studio of hers, miles and miles of it!

"Walk erect," said Mme. Stabile, "never stiffly."

She would shock me by shouting at the top of her voice: *"Culo dentro, pancia dentro!"* In other words, backside in, belly in!

I can still hear that cry of hers as I marched across her carpet, to the rhythm of her handclapping: *"Culo dentro, pancia dentro,* Robertuccia!"

It was such a pitifully small studio to stage grand opera in.

I remember how for the "Mad Scene" Mme. Stabile tried to picture what the Metropolitan stage looked like at that point.

"Imagine a big staircase," she would say, pointing to one corner of the small and narrow room.

I had to imagine a great deal.

I was with Mme. Stabile from 1944 to 1950. I have several dictionaries that she gave me as gifts. One of them I treasure above all others. It is dated Christmas 1947, and carries the following inscription:

> *Alla mia Robertina, con immenso affetto, e che la dolce lingua la guidi e l'inspiri sul cammino del arte e sul sentiero della gloria.*
>
> > *L'Affezionata tua maestra,*
> > ANTONIETTA STABILE.*

In another book she wrote: *"Non dimenticarmi mai. Io ti voglio tanto bene."* "Don't ever forget me. I love you so much."

And I, in turn, had come to love Mme. Stabile as a second mother; in fact, I called her my *mamma spirituale.*

I was with Mme. Stabile all those years of preparation. We had our language and our librettos, our *scenas* and our talks, our Dante and Petrarch and Pirandello.

She was always so certain that I would make the grade. It was an added voice of encouragement and support during that unending routine of study, study, study.

Well, when I finally made my Metropolitan debut, Mme. Stabile could not come.

The poor darling had decided that her Robertuccia would need a bigger room to be coached in now that she was a full-fledged member of the Metropolitan Opera Company.

---

* "To my Robertina, with great affection and hopes that our sweet language will guide and inspire her along the path of art and on the road to glory.

> "Your affectionate teacher,
> Antonietta Stabile."

She rented a larger studio, and the first day she entered her new quarters she slipped on the freshly shellacked floor and broke her hip.

So, when I came out to sing Zerlina on Friday, November 17, 1950, my *mamma spirituale* was at home in a wheelchair.

5

"I'm in, Mom!"

Age: 19

A STUDIO expression I learned very early as a singer was "to go out." It did not mean simply to open a door and leave, nor did it mean to have a date with a steady boyfriend. For us in the studio it had a very special meaning: "To go out" meant you were out in the professional world, on your own, *singing before the public.* You were launched.

I had been studying with Mr. Herman for seven years. During all that time I had been privately tutored in French, German, and Italian. I now knew twenty operas cold. Can you blame me for beginning to wonder when, if ever, I was going "to go out" and show what, if anything, I could do? I was nineteen, and frankly I was thinking of myself as getting on in years. Other pupils of Mr. Herman were already making the grade. Patrice Munsel was singing everywhere. Another one of our coloraturas had gone to Italy, and we were receiving wonderful reports about her. That fine American basso Norman Scott had finally come through. They had all "gone out"—all but little me. I just kept on coming for another lesson—and there I was, yearning to go out, to do opera, to sing, and to be heard by lots of people. I went on wondering and waiting and getting a little impatient.

"Patience, patience," Mr. Herman would say with a knowing smile. "Learning how to wait is half the battle in music, Roberta. It's just a question of time—and timing."

The "timing" came sooner than expected, and again it was Jan Peerce who set the clock for us. He had come to work on some things with Mr. Herman. One day he heard me sing, and he must have been impressed, for the next day he went to see Mr. Hurok.

"Sol," I understand he told him, "I want you to hear this kid. She's terrific!"

"Everybody's *terrific*," said Mr. Hurok. "Can't they just be *good?* I'm busy, Jan.... Okay, okay, where do you want me to hear her?"

"Up at Bill Herman's studio."

"All right—and she'd better be good. Never mind the 'terrific.' "

Mr. Herman preferred not to be present when Mr. Hurok and Mr. Peerce arrived. Once he explained to me that when others were brought in to hear me, it was psychologically better for him not to be around; I think he meant better for him, for me, and for the "others."

So I did the audition for Sol Hurok in Bill Herman's studio. I sang the "Mad Scene" from Thomas' *Hamlet,* the aria, "Ombra leggiera," from Meyerbeer's *Dinorah,* and "Una voce poco fà" from Rossini's *Barber of Seville.* Without showing it, I was crushed. I didn't think I did well at all. I ran into a little vocal trouble on the extremely high notes. They weren't too clear. A few of them sounded muffled to me, and a little pinched. Even while I was singing, it seemed to me that everything I had ever done wrong gathered up and came out of me that day. And at a time like that! I had never sung for anyone as important as Mr. Hurok. All through my student days Mr. Herman had shied away from letting professional people hear me. It was part of his "timing."

There was a brief silence after my last note. Then Mr. Hurok, a stocky, bland, well-groomed man of affable manner, spoke.

"Well, maybe operetta. Maybe we could do something along that line . . . provided you studied and made up your mind to try out for it."

I didn't like that one bit.

"But I want opera, Mr. Hurok."

"Opera! My dear child, you'd spend the rest of your life warming the bench. Who's going to give you a chance? After all, you're just a beginner."

I must have been even worse than I feared.

"But I want only opera," I insisted. "That's what I've worked for all these seven years, Mr. Hurok. That's what I enjoy. That's what I can do, and that's what I want."

Mr. Hurok seemed a little taken aback by my outburst. He sighed and shrugged his shoulders. That was as far as he was prepared to commit himself—operetta and "maybe," at that. Finally he and Mr. Peerce left, and Mr. Peerce later related to me how, as they walked to the corner, Mr. Hurok had turned to him and asked,

"Well, Jan, what do you think?"

"She's marvelous!"

Mr. Hurok looked at him in surprise. He still wouldn't commit himself.

"I don't know," he said cagily. "Yes, I suppose she's good . . ."

They walked a little farther in silence.

". . . But who knows, Jan. . . . there are so many of them, so many disappointments, so much risk. . . . Still, maybe there's a chance . . . not much, mind you, but a chance."

Mr. Peerce said nothing.

"You can't tell," Mr. Hurok went on, as if to himself. "She needs experience. . . . On the other hand . . ."

Mr. Peerce let him sound himself out.

Anyway, Mr. Hurok was a little doubtful both ways, but I guess Jan finally persuaded him that I was worth taking a chance on. That was on the street corner . . .

At that precise moment, back in Bill Herman's studio, a would-be coloratura was crying her heart out. Nobody had to tell me I hadn't done well. A great opportunity had come and I had muffed it. My mind kept dwelling on that high note in the Rossini aria. It came back like a stab of conscience. It had been squeezed thin and undernourished, and I hadn't held it long enough, almost as if there were nothing to hold onto. The note had come out all right, but it hadn't stayed out long enough. I hadn't made it what it should have been to impress a man like Sol Hurok—a "wham" note.

Luckily Mr. Herman was there to console me as best he could.

"I'm positive you're magnifying a triviality," he said. "Let's wait and see how right you are—or how wrong."

So we waited. One day passed and then another. Not a word from Mr. Hurok. I knew I was right. When a whole week had gone by and we hadn't heard a thing, I reminded Mr. Herman that I was right. I had not magnified a triviality. I had been bad and Mr. Hurok knew it. I tried not to brood over it. If I had been bad, I just had to make up my mind to be better the next time—if there was to be a next time. I had to work harder—to perfect the high notes, the phrasing, everything. Otherwise I didn't stand the ghost of a chance, not with all the competition around.

It must have been the eighth or ninth day after the audition. I came to the studio to find a beaming and self-satisfied Bill Herman.

"Mae Frohman just called me from the Hurok office," he said.

I caught a tinge of mocking triumph in his voice.

"She said Mr. Hurok would like a certain young lady to come down to Town Hall tomorrow to sing for his booking agents. ... Take it all back?"

I scarcely believed him. There was one tiny catch, however. Mr. Herman told me that Edwin Lester, of operetta fame, was to be there, too. That brought an immediate echo of Mr. Hurok's words, "Well, maybe operetta." I winced, but said nothing. I could not have been so bad, after all, not if Mr. Hurok's booking staff was going to hear me in the main song-recital hall in New York.

Then something dawned on both of us. *I had never sung in a big hall in my life!* Mr. Herman, my teacher for seven years, had never heard me anywhere but in his studio. Neither of us had any idea how I would sound in a large auditorium. We knew that that was the very first thing we had to take care of—and on that very day. We just had to find ourselves a large hall for me to sing in. Now that wasn't at all easy. To begin with, we couldn't rent one of the size we wanted on such short notice, and even if we could, it would have been far too expensive. Carnegie Hall was completely out of the question.

We were just about at our wits' end when Mr. Herman thought of the pianist who came regularly to the studio to accompany me. He was a fine Negro musician by the name of Henry Smith. Mr. Smith lived in Newark, New Jersey, and belonged to a Baptist church there. Mr. Herman promptly communicated with Mr. Smith, and between them they arranged that somehow or other Mr. Smith's church in Newark, New Jersey, was the place I was going to try out my voice in before tomorrow's audition in Town Hall. Arrangements were immediately made for us to have the use of the church at eight P.M. This was the first week in January of 1950.

Four of us—Mr. Herman, Mr. Smith, my mother, and I—took the train to Newark. I shall never forget that evening. It was freezing. We arrived a little early and found that services were still going on in Mr. Smith's church. Next to the church was a small hardware store. While we were shivering in the cold out on the street, we looked through the store window and saw a large stove burning snugly in the middle of the store. With one thought, the four of us went inside, and the owner very kindly invited us to warm ourselves at the stove. So there we stood chatting away and warming our hands at the stove. We spent about fifteen minutes in the hardware store, thanked the owner, and finally marched into the church next door.

Mr. Smith took his place at the piano. Mother occupied a seat in the front row and Mr. Herman sat in the very last row of the church, to be as far from my voice as he could get. The first thing I sang was the aria that Mr. Hurok had expressed a desire to hear me sing, the aria of the Queen of the Night from Mozart's *The Magic Flute*. After that, I sang "Una voce poco fà" and the "Ombra leggiera" from *Dinorah*. Finally, I did a few songs, ending with "The Last Rose of Summer."

For a while the only people in the church were Mr. Herman, Mr. Smith, my mother, and myself. For a while . . . As I went on singing, without my noticing it, a band of little children began filing into the church and noiselessly taking seats in the back and listening to me. When I had finished, I was almost startled to see these beaming little children trooping down the aisle of the church and crying out to me in their bright, cheery voices:

"Who are you?"

"Please, please, sing some more, won't you?"

"What a beautiful voice you have!"

"Right from heaven!"

All this from the first real audience I had ever sung to.

I was so overwhelmed that all I could think of saying was:

"Oh, thank you, thank you so much! I didn't know anyone was listening!"

Of course, Mr. Herman had been listening very intently from the back of the church. I waited for his verdict eagerly. He had always been honest with me—honest when he thought me good and honest when he thought me not so good. I knew he wouldn't hold back now.

"I think it will be all right," he said simply. "It's not *too* big, Roberta, but it carries. You must keep remembering to project."

It wasn't exactly overwhelming, but it was good enough for me. I knew what I had to do, and I had learned to gauge bigger distances. The "not *too* big" hurt a little, but it was the truth, and the truth is always a good place to start from. I had now put two serious hurdles behind me. I had finally sung in a large place and my teacher said my voice carried. We had had quite a scare and it was now behind us. It was about eleven o'clock when we bundled up tightly and went out into the cold again. I went straight to bed when we got home and the same thing happened that always happens before an important day: I didn't sleep a wink all night.

The audition in Town Hall was to be at two. Again Mr. Herman preferred not to be present.

"I don't want to be in the way," he said.

I began to insist, till I remembered how he had always wanted it that way.

"Any last instructions?"

Mr. Herman brought up the palms of his hands gently.

"Don't think of anything. Just sing. Keep your mind on two things and two things only: the words and the music. Above all, try to avoid thinking of anything technical."

I nodded agreement. "Anything more?"

He smiled. "You've got nothing to worry about."

I arrived early at Town Hall so that I could try out my voice before the others came. Those few minutes with my accompanist were very precious. They gave me added confidence and a chance to size up the acoustics of the hall. Then doors began to open and close, and one by one they filed in—managers, assistant managers, booking agents, out-of-town representatives. I was appalled at how many of them had come just to hear me, all very practical hard-boiled businessmen of music. They were going to see whether Roberta Peters, the professional name I had taken, had something they could sell. . . . I saw the kindly but slightly worried face of Mae Frohman among them and flashed her a reassuring smile.

I knew this was my big chance and that, no matter how Mr. Herman might later minimize it, I couldn't afford to bungle it. I began to sing. I was nervous, but only for a while. When finally I warmed up I knew I was doing all right, much better than when Mr. Hurok had heard me in the studio. I could tell they were interested before I even heard or saw their response. It's something you learn to sense very early in the game. And I realized how helpful our trip to Newark had been the night before.

I started off with "Caro nome" from Verdi's *Rigoletto* and followed up with arias by Mozart, Rossini, and Meyerbeer. I tried to remember what Miss Frohman had cautioned: "Sing what they already know; don't try anything new on them." I added two French songs that I was sure they would know, and of course the song that is a kind of luck charm to me— "Bonnie Sweet Bessie." In my diary entry of that day I am embarrassed to find these words: "They were really amazed. I socked them! I knocked them right out of their seats!"

Yet I really think I did. After it was over, they all came up to the stage with big smiles on their faces and congratulated me in the warmest terms. Nicest of all was the compliment of

Mr. Bottorf of the National Concert Artists' Corporation. In a tone of mocking reproach, he said, "Look here, young lady, I was supposed to leave for Boston an hour ago." Then he added in a cajoling voice, "If you've got just one more little song like the last one, Miss Peters, I'd like to hear it."

Edwin Lester, my friend the operetta man, also seemed deeply impressed—with reservations.

"You lean too far forward when you sing," he said, "and your dramatics can stand improvement. Do you mind trying one or two songs my way?" And he showed me what "his way" was.

I sang two songs with my body at the improved angle. Mr. Lester appeared to be satisfied, and of course he began talking operetta again.

"Have you ever read lines? Do you know any operetta?"

He was so sweet that I didn't have the heart to tell him again that I didn't want operetta.

I WANTED OPERA!

The report of the audition must have reached Mr. Herman fast, for later at the studio I could read it on his face before he said a word. Mr. Peerce was again there that afternoon. I remember he called up Miss Frohman, and she told him they were still sitting around in Mr. Hurok's office talking about me.

"Now is the time to talk terms to them," said Mr. Peerce. He seemed suddenly to think of something. Reaching in his pocket, he brought out a ticket.

"One standing-room ticket for tonight's *Rigoletto* at the Metropolitan," he said. "To be used by Roberta Peters, the new Gilda. Not transferable."

I think I did Mr. Herman proud that day.

Later, at home, Miss Frohman telephoned to tell me how delighted she was that everything went so well. I was waiting for something more concrete than that, but that was as far as she would go.

"I'll call you after I've talked to Mr. Hurok again," she said. That could only mean one thing—more waiting.

That night I used Mr. Peerce's standing-room ticket. It was only during "Caro nome" that I realized, with a strange new thrill, that I had sung it myself only a few hours earlier in Town Hall, and that if all went well, I might some day be standing up there on the stage instead of where I was, during a Metropolitan performance of *Rigoletto*.

So I waited. The whole next morning went without a word from the Hurok office. I began getting fidgety. Finally, in midafternoon, the telephone rang. I literally pounced on it. It was Mae Frohman very casually asking whether I would be available the following day to come down to the Metropolitan.

"Max Rudolf would like to hear you sing. . . ."

I managed to splutter out: "Why, of course I'll be available!"

"They want to hear the Queen of the Night aria, and bring along the usual coloratura repertory."

"Anything special?"

"Yes, bring the whole score of *Rigoletto*. . . ."

"Oh?"

"Just in case Mr. Rudolf wants to hear more than 'Caro nome.' "

Naturally there was no sleep for me that night. I tossed around and never once closed my eyes. I must have looked a sight when at three thirty the following afternoon I walked into the Metropolitan Opera House, marched up the stairs to the grand tier, and strode into the Ladies Parlor, where Mr. Rudolf was going to hear me sing. It was raining out and I was wearing my galoshes. Mother was with me.

The room was sparsely furnished—a large concert grand, a couch, a few chairs, a wardrobe of sorts, and several coat hangers. Miss Frohman stepped forward to introduce me and my mother to Mr. Rudolf, who immediately went to the piano. There was very little talking beyond the usual preliminaries. As Mr. Rudolf accompanied, I sang the second aria of the Queen of the Night from Mozart's *Magic Flute*. It is the aria with the high F's. When I finished, I glanced at Mr. Rudolf. All he said was "Very nice."

I could see from the smile on his face that he was pleased, but how pleased I couldn't tell.

"What operas do you know?" he asked.

"I've studied twenty and—"

"Twenty operas!" he cried out, his calm momentarily shattered. "Do you mean to say twenty *complete* operas?"

"Yes, Mr. Rudolf."

"Hm . . . and the acting too?"

I said, "Yes," and again he said, "Hm."

Then he asked me who my teacher was, and when I told him, he nodded.

"What opera score did you bring with you?"

"*Rigoletto.*"

"Good, but we won't do 'Caro nome'—not just yet," he said. "Suppose we start with the duet in the second act, the one with the Duke . . ."

So I began singing—bits of this and bits of that, and in between a few words of comment or criticism. I soon suspected what Mr. Rudolf was listening for most of all. He wanted to see how I took his criticism. From his questions I could tell he was also interested in what general ideas I had about the opera I was singing. He was also watching my phrasing very carefully. There always was a little conversation between arias and fragments of arias. I thought to myself, "This is more like a coaching lesson than an audition."

About a certain phrase in the duet Mr. Rudolf would ask: "Now tell me, Miss Peters, how would you do it? Should it be pianissimo? Would you give it a little more body at this point?"

I suppose he wanted to see whether I had ideas of my own, or whether I was just a puppet.

"Now let's hear your 'Caro nome,' Miss Peters," he said. "Just the end of it, if you don't mind."

I could see that he was very pleased when I took the high E at the end.

"It's not generally done here these days and we don't demand it, of course." But I could see he loved that note.

I was with Mr. Rudolf almost a full hour. Finally he rose from the piano and came over to me. Very quietly, spacing out his phrases, he said:

"We'll let you know.... It looks very good.... Keep on working.... I'm very pleased.... We'll be in touch with Miss Frohman.... Very nice."

That was all. I had never met Max Rudolf before, so I couldn't quite size up his impression at the moment, though I had every reason to believe that it was good.

Before leaving the Metropolitan, I had a few minutes alone with Miss Frohman. I was curious to know how she had arranged the audition with Mr. Rudolf so quickly, what she could possibly have told him about me.

"To begin with, they have a very high regard for Mr. Hurok...."

"So I understand. Go on."

"Well, I reminded Mr. Rudolf that we'd never sent him anyone who we didn't think was ready."

"That was nice," I said. "Anything more?"

"That we had great confidence in you ..."

"And ... ?"

"He asked me what you were like."

"What did you say? Please don't hold anything back."

"That you were very fresh, very pure, and very rare."

"Wow!" I said. "I'll bet he's already changed his mind about the Hurok office."

"Fishing, Miss Peters?" said Miss Frohman.

"You're a darling!" I said.

So Mother and I climbed into a cab and rushed up to the studio, where a very anxious Bill Herman was pacing the floor nervously. I had to tell him everything—how I sang, what I sang, and how I thought Mr. Rudolf reacted. After giving a breathless account of it all, I paused to take a deep breath.

"I think I did well, Bill," I said.

That was all he needed. He was all smiles. He knew if I said so, it was so, and there was nothing to worry about. I have always been my severest critic, more severe than even Bill Herman himself, who never spared me when I had it coming.

"That's fine!" he said. "Now suppose we go over what he said, point by point." And we celebrated the best way we knew how—by working. That was Friday. Before I left, I asked Mr. Herman what I should do over the weekend.

"Just relax," he said.

Which is exactly what I did, till Tuesday morning, January 24, when Miss Frohman called. In what I suspect was a carefully rehearsed nonchalance, she asked,

"Could you be ready for an audition tomorrow at four... for Mr. Bing...on the stage of the Metropolitan?"

I gasped.

"Why, yes, yes, of course!"

I didn't know what to say, I was so flabbergasted. Rudolf Bing had been appointed the new General Manager, though he wasn't to take over till the new season began. Having just come from Europe, he was getting his bearings around the Metropolitan while Edward Johnson completed his last year there. If I recall, Mr. Bing was listening to many of the artists, not the first-string artists, but the others, as well as an occasional newcomer, and the chorus.

"What do you think I should sing?" I asked Miss Frohman.

"Mr. Rudolf wants you to sing the two Queen of the Night arias and 'Una voce poco fà.'"

This is what I wrote in my diary that night:

I'm really looking forward to it. I know I'm ready. And as long as I feel well, I know I'll do well. Mother, I can see, is very nervous, and Dad too. I tried to get to bed early but I couldn't. I'm going to wear my "audition dress" —the purple taffeta skirt and the white blouse. I'm all ready. I'll feel much better tomorrow night. It is a big step. *And it is all happening so fast!"*

I got to the Metropolitan promptly at four. I came in through the executive entrance right off Eighth Avenue on the Thirty-ninth Street side of the house. I sat in a corner of the little cubicle of a room just outside the press office—and waited. The place was just buzzing. Singers, musicians, officials, secretaries all scurried by, often greeting one another in French, German, or Italian. And I just sat in my little corner, noiseless and awed. Finally someone called out my name and I was led through a door, up a short flight of stairs, and along a narrow passageway.

Almost before I knew it, I was walking on the stage of the Metropolitan Opera House! As I came through the wings I saw Paula Lenchner, Carmen Grazia, and Lois Hunt standing to one side in a little group. They looked at me as I passed. I think they were going to sing for Mr. Bing, too. Lots of people were milling around, and there, at the piano, waiting to accompany for me, was Walter Taussig.

I was glad to have Mr. Taussig for two reasons. On Mr. Herman's recommendation, I had been going to him for the last seven years to work over all my German and French operas. Then, he had just been engaged by the Metropolitan. Mr. Taussig knew my repertory very well, though I hadn't had an opportunity of going over it with him before coming to the Metropolitan that afternoon.

I began with the second aria of the Queen of the Night from *The Magic Flute*—again the one with the high F's. They were giving *Faust* that night at the Metropolitan, and the stage set of the first act was up, which was good for me. My voice was able to project against the set, instead of drifting into an empty background.

I got through the aria, and I suppose I was scared, but only in a way. Not scared in myself. You see, I didn't know I was scared. I was too numb. I somehow pushed the thought from me what a great thing it was to be standing on the stage of the Metropolitan—and singing. I must have lulled myself with a sort of self-delusion that this was just another audition. Subconsciously, I had covered up the scare by walking on the stage with a real show of confidence. I had said to myself that I had a job to do. That job was to sing. For that job I had trained for seven long years. I said to myself, "I am going to sing as well as I know how. And that's about all anybody can expect me to do."

I finished the aria, and they asked me to repeat it. No comments, no applause, nothing; just a request to do the aria again. It was then that I noticed that Mr. Bing had changed his seat. I could see him now in one of the boxes. I thought, "He wants to hear what the aria sounds like from different parts of the house." I repeated the aria.

"Well, now, relax," I heard Mr. Rudolf say to me from the orchestra, "that's over."

So we both thought. But Mr. Bing must have moved to still another location. I couldn't see where he was this time, but he somehow signaled to Mr. Rudolf, who again turned up to me and, in a rather remorseful tone, said:

"Do you mind singing that aria once more, Miss Peters?"

Of course I didn't mind. . . . It was then that I realized more and more people were coming into the auditorium. I could tell from the light that came into the hall as the side doors opened.

I sang the aria for the third time. There was a pause, and Mr. Rudolf looked up again.

"What else have you brought along with you, Miss Peters?"

"'Una voce poco fà.'"

"Fine! That's in a different vein. Let's hear you do it."

I sang the Rossini aria.

"Thank you," said Mr. Rudolf, "now just relax for a minute."

I did, and after two or three minutes I heard his voice again. It was a voice of humble apology.

"Miss Peters, if you have any more high F's left, would you mind doing the Queen of the Night aria over again? This is positively the last time—I hope."

I laughed and said, "Of course not, Mr. Rudolf. I'd be very happy to sing it for you as often as you like."

I subsequently learned that among the people who had slipped into the house when those side doors opened were the conductors Fritz Reiner, Fritz Stiedry, and Wilfred Pelletier, and the stage director, Mr. Yannopoulos. That explained why I was asked to repeat the aria so often.

After I sang it for the fourth time—with all my high F's where they should be—Mr. Rudolf merely said, "Thank you."

As I walked off the stage, a tall, slender, ascetic-looking man with a suave manner greeted me. It was Rudolf Bing, the new General Manager of the Metropolitan.

"Well, young lady," he said, "it was very nice."

"Thank you, Mr. Bing."

"You realize, of course, that you must not be exploited."

I think Mr. Bing was worried from the beginning that there might be a temptation to overplay me if I suddenly made the grade.

"Of course, Mr. Bing, I realize that," I said. "My only ambition is to be a good worker. I've always enjoyed working and I hope to work seriously in the future."

"That's the right spirit."

"I will not let anyone exploit me—not anyone, Mr. Bing."

"Good!" he said. "Then we needn't say anything more about that. You realize, too, that if we engage you, you must work slowly and conscientiously."

"Yes, Mr. Bing."

"We want you to grow in the theater. We want you to watch and sit around and get the feeling of the opera stage. As often as you can, you must watch the other singers work."

And I said, "Mr. Bing, I realize I have a long way to go, but I'm willing to work and study and make myself worthy. ... Now may I ask you a question, Mr. Bing?"

"Naturally."

"How do you like my voice?"

I could see from the look on his face that it wasn't what he had expected.

"That *is* a direct question, Miss Peters," he said sternly, and I felt ashamed of myself for asking him. Then he smiled for the first time, as if to reassure me, and laughed.

"Good-bye, Miss Peters," he said.

"Good-bye, Mr. Bing."

Until I saw that smile and heard him laugh, I found him rather austere and cold. I knew this was a serious man who took his work seriously. He would expect the same of everyone working for him.

Mother and I left the Metropolitan the same way we had come in—on the Thirty-ninth-Street side—and took a cab to Mr. Herman's studio. As I stepped out of the cab, a strange intuition made me look up the facade of the house.

Sure enough, there was Mr. Herman hanging out the window waiting for me to give him a sign. I raised my right hand and brought my thumb and index finger together in a gesture of satisfaction, as if to say, "Don't look so anxious. It went fine. I'll give you all the details later. There's nothing to worry about."

I could see the look of relief spread over his face before his head withdrew.

Mother and I flew upstairs and told him everything. After I had finished answering a thousand questions and gone over every detail of the audition a dozen times, in came Jan Peerce, bursting for news. And I had to repeat the whole thing over again, and still again a few hours later—to Dad.

I shall always remember Wednesday, January 25, 1950, as my day of repetition. Four deliveries of the Queen of the Night aria and at least three of the story of my Metropolitan audition. Oh, what talk, talk, talk that day!

While I was at Mr. Herman's studio, the Hurok office called to say they were very pleased. Miss Frohman had not been to the audition, but she said Martin Feinstein, also of Mr. Hurok's office, had sat next to Mr. Reiner in the house.

"And . . . ?" I asked.

"It looks good," was all Miss Frohman would say.

I wanted to ask a dozen questions, but I suspected that wasn't the thing to do, not at this point. Miss Frohman must have realized the state I was in.

"Things look very good, Miss Peters," she said. "We'll keep in touch with you."

For several days that was all. They telephoned, repeated that "things looked good," and completely tightened up. I heard absolutely nothing more. Mr. Bing went back to Europe and Roberta Peters went on studying—music, languages, coaching—and keeping fit. Finally, I gave up thinking about the Metropolitan altogether. It was almost as if it had never happened—like a fading dream.

Hardly anyone outside my immediate family circle, Mr. Herman, and the Hurok office, knew about the audition. A day later I did tell my Italian teacher, Mme. Stabile, but then she was my *mamma spirituale* and I her *Robertuccia*. She was in the family. I said nothing to my German and French teachers, however. While it was brewing, we all thought it best to keep as quiet as possible about it. After all, no one was sure how it would work out, and whether I would just be filed away with hundreds of other names in the deep recesses of the Metropolitan index system. They might decide they didn't need me or that I was too young and inexperienced. . . . I went to my lessons the same as before, as if nothing had happened. Mr. Herman, bless him, never referred to it.

Once he said, "Whether anything comes of it or not, don't worry about it. If not now, then certainly later. Remember, it's only a question of time." That was all.

I gathered that he wanted me to feel that if I didn't make the Metropolitan right then and there, it wouldn't be fatal. Over the years he had instilled in me a healthy psychology of waiting, and, while waiting, going about the business of being fully prepared when the waiting finally came to an end.

Weeks went by.

One morning, late in March, the telephone rang. It was Miss Frohman again, and I waited patiently to be told once more that "it looked good." Instead she asked me to come down to the office, and again I knew better than to ask why. Mother didn't go with me this time. She had some shopping to do and we arranged to meet in Child's Restaurant, across the street from the Hurok office.

After I was announced, I opened the door to Miss Frohman's office, and there she was, holding a letter against her chest.

"Read this."

I came up close and saw it was a letter from the Metropolitan. I peered still closer and read just one line: "We are very happy to accept Miss Peters for the season of 1950–51."

That was all I needed. I spluttered a few words of thanks to Miss Frohman, and went bounding out of the office like a wild filly. I took the elevator, flew across the street and almost got run over, and dashed into Child's, where mother was waiting. She didn't have to be told. The thrill of it was written all over me.

"I'm in, Mom!"

And that was the greatest reward of all, to see my mother's dream come true on her face as it lit up with pride and joy. I knew then that no matter what lay ahead, nothing would ever quite equal the beauty of this moment. It was the happiest day in my life, and the proudest in Mother's.

6

"Please Report for Rehearsal"

Age: 20

FOR three or four days, I guess I just walked around with my head in the clouds. I was now "Roberta Peters, Metropolitan soprano." That wild, arrogant dream of a thirteen-year-old kid had really come true. Then, on the fifth or sixth day, it suddenly struck me like lightning: Nothing had been said about any actual performance. Not a word about when or how I would begin to sing. I was in the Metropolitan, but I evidently still had to prove I belonged there. And I could only prove it by singing a role—by making my debut and making it good. Nobody had said anything about that at all. So, naturally, I had a talk with Miss Frohman.

"Mr. Rudolf didn't say anything about performances," she said, "except, possibly, for a slight chance that you may do the Queen of the Night on January 12, 1951. . . ."

"January 12, 1951! But that's a whole year off!"

"I know, but that's the way it is. And even so, I wouldn't count on it. It's too far ahead to really promise anything. . . .

And, for God's sake, hold your horses! You've a whole life-time before you."

"What do I do meanwhile?"

"Do? Plenty. What they want you to do is to go on studying —studying as you've never studied before. Work and coach and listen and take in everything . . . and wait. . . ."

"Here we go again," I said. "That's been my leading role so far—waiting."

"And while you're waiting, drink it all in—the music, the acting, the staging, the costumes—the whole Metropolitan Opera House, inside and out."

"Where do we begin?"

"Begin where you left off, as if nothing had happened. Go on working the way you were, only harder . . . and when the warm weather comes, give yourself a vacation."

So I worked till the end of June, and then I took my first real long vacation since I had begun studying—my first in eight years. All I had had up to then was a week or so in the open, always close to New York. This time I wanted something different. I spent four whole weeks in Provincetown. I studied painting and drank beer and played tennis and went swimming. . . .

I simply forgot I was a singer. I forgot all about the Metropolitan, the singing lessons, the drama coaching, the languages. I was just a vacationer. I did everything I hadn't done before and had always wanted to do. I even had a few dates. I had a gloriously lazy time in the sun and water. I wanted to pack into those four weeks in Provincetown eight long years of pent-up play and idleness. I was being a girl again and loving every moment of it.

After that came a week of heavenly music—at the Berkshire Festival in Tanglewood. No singing, just listening. Finally I got back to New York and wound up my vacation with a week at Rockaway Beach. There I drank in the sun and plunged in the invigorating salt water. Then I came home, all rested, and ready to start work, and there awaiting me was a letter from Max Rudolf. I tore it open excitedly.

It was a very polite letter, I must say. It began by "assuming" that I knew all about the Katherine Turney Long courses which the Metropolitan Opera was sponsoring for young singers, particularly singers who had just signed up with the company. Wouldn't I be interested in taking them? I would have the benefit of Metropolitan coaches like Barbini and Cellini, of stage directors like Dino Yannopoulous and Herbert Graf, of conductors like Fritz Busch and Kurt Adler ... and Max Leavitt would also be giving a course in acting that might be profitable to me.

The letter was very courteously phrased. It was all in a casual tone of suggestion. Nothing firm or imperative about it. But I sensed it was a diplomatic command. I knew that if Mr. Rudolf thought that the courses would be good for me, there must be some reason for it and he wouldn't expect me to say No. And for me to say No would have implied I had a pretty high opinion of myself. I felt funny about it at first. I didn't like its implications one bit. "Who would be hearing me?" I said to myself. "I'll be singing the way I've always been singing—to the studio wall." I had studied twenty complete operas—to what purpose? To start school again? And I wasn't even being asked to prepare for a performance. I wanted a real audience! I was a soprano under contract with the Metropolitan and here they were asking me to become a student. That's how impatient I was to get going—and how silly and conceited, too.

So my first impulse was to turn down Mr. Rudolf's proposal that I enroll for the courses. If I wasn't going to get a real performance and a houseful of listeners, I could wait and meanwhile study by myself and with Bill Herman, the way I had been doing for so many years. Why a school for acting, any-

way? Hadn't I been coached thoroughly? Didn't I know the
action of twenty whole operas in great detail? Hadn't I been
acting out operatic parts since I was ten? It was a very in-
dignant coloratura who walked into Bill Herman's studio the
following day.

"I'll be singing to the walls," I said at the end of my tirade.

"Don't worry," he said, trying to mollify me. "Haven't you
heard? Even the walls have ears."

From which I gathered that my first impulse was wrong
and that, for more reasons than he cared to enumerate, he
thought it best for me to answer Mr. Rudolf in the affirmative
and thank him for the thoughtful suggestion. Mr. Herman was
certainly right, because it was from these courses that the
Metropolitan first became confident that they could safely
call on me as a last-minute substitute when the emergency
came. For one thing, it was in one of Dr. Graf's courses that
autumn that I worked out Zerlina so thoroughly that I could
step into a performance of *Don Giovanni* on a moment's notice,
if the need arose.

The courses ran from September 5 to October 13, a few
short weeks before the opening of the Metropolitan season.
The school was maintained at the company's expense, and those
enrolled could go over anything in the repertory of the following season and whatever else they desired. During the first
three weeks I worked on Zerlina, Rosina, and the Queen of
the Night.

Later I went over some other operas I had been studying,
even though they weren't scheduled by the Met. I did Bellini's *La Sonnambula* and Auber's *Fra Diavolo,* both of which
I had first studied with Mr. Herman several years earlier. It
was good for me to go over them again and it was good for
the Met to know that I could do them. With Mr. Yannopoulos
I worked on Zerbinetta's aria from Richard Strauss's *Ariadne
auf Naxos*. That, too, I had already studied, and for me it

is one of the trickiest of all arias. I sang it for Mr. Yannopoulos in the original version. Later Strauss rewrote it, because he was told it was too difficult to sing.

Then I had Max Leavitt. At first we all thought he was slightly on the eccentric side because of what he wanted us to do. His course was the only one involving group study. The very first thing he asked us was to portray an action of some kind without saying a word. The rest of us were to guess from the pantomime what that action was. It was like a charade. Of course, we all thought it kindergarten stuff at first. I remember the idea I chose. I was sweeping a floor with a broom, picking up the dust and putting the broom back in the closet. Only there was no broom, no dust, and no closet. Props were strictly forbidden. I was such a brilliant actress that when I had finished, several voices cried out in unison:

"You were in a rowboat!"

"You were digging a hole in the ground!"

"You were out picking berries!"

I couldn't believe it! I thought I had made my pantomime as clear as day. When I told them what I thought I was doing, they all burst out laughing, and I must have got as red as a beet. I had never been taught to do anything like that before, and for the first time I realized what a long road I still had to travel before I could call myself an actress. Luckily, I wasn't the only one who couldn't portray something without having it mistaken for a hole in the ground. The laugh was on all of us that day. And of course we changed our minds about Mr. Leavitt.

Very respectfully we listened to the little sermon he gave us on what he thought was the secret of all gestures and pantomime. The motions must not only flow naturally from the thought but from one another, too. It made me conscious of what to do with my hands and how to control my body—to have my body do what I wanted it to do for me, and not the

other way around. I had studied this with Mme. Stabile, but
Mr. Leavitt made me see that there was still work, lots and
lots of work, to be done.

Far from thinking it was a ridiculous waste of time, I now
realized it would be very valuable to me, and I'm the kind of
person who likes to listen to all kinds of advice. I take everything with a grain of salt, of course, but I always wind up
getting something good out of it—provided I explore it enough.
Later Mr. Leavitt himself gave us the ideas to work out in
pantomime.

"You're a bus driver," he would say. "Now, how would you
go about driving this bus? What would you do with your
hands?"

And we tried to give him the pantomime, the bus being a
chair.

"Now, let's eat dinner out in a restaurant."

It was amazing how difficult it was, without eating utensils
or a table, with nothing but a chair, to pretend to be eating a
whole dinner. And, I might add, no dinner there to eat. Mr.
Leavitt showed us how to envision the whole action. There
was a real technique to it: Let the idea evolve far enough
ahead, flowing one action into the next. It taught us how to
develop line and continuity.

Then he gave us parts to read, little scenes with dialogue.
I was given a scene from *Death of a Salesman* and another
from *Rain*. That was the first half of the course. By the time
it was through, I knew I had gained a great deal from it. The
second half was much easier, at least for me. This involved
all sorts of physical exercises, most of which the others had
never done before. I had been going to a gymnasium for years,
so I was elected monitor. My job was to think up the exercises
and to do them in consecutive order with the class: One
routine, for instance, would be that of sitting on the floor,
rolling, and walking in a sitting position.

As the courses advanced into the autumn, I realized more and more what Mr. Herman had meant. The walls did have ears! Especially when I sang duets with Thomas Hayward in *Rigoletto* in Dr. Graf's class, and also when I did the "La ci darem la mano" scene from *Don Giovanni* with Larry Davidson. The walls must have been spying for Mr. Bing. . . . Once the gentleman did his own spying, with rather dire results.

We were in the midst of a scene from *The Marriage of Figaro* one afternoon when, without warning, the door opened and Mr. Bing entered. We just froze. Our singing was suddenly stiff and self-conscious. We had all been doing fine up to that point. Just as suddenly as he had come, Mr. Bing left. The change back to the way we had been singing was so noticeable that we all stopped and started to laugh.

I see that my diary entry of Thursday, October 5, 1950, records a similar visit by Max Rudolf. It happened during our class with Dr. Graf.

Larry Davidson and I worked on *Don Giovanni* today," I wrote. "I did 'Batti, batti'—recitative before and after, and the ensuing duet. Who should walk in? Mr. Rudolf. He began to conduct. I took the second half ('Pace, pace') a little too fast, and he told me so. It should be the same as 'Batti, batti.' Also it is very disconcerting when one is working on acting for the first lesson to sing full voice. And when Rudolf or any other *gros bonnet* comes in, *one must sing*. At regular rehearsals it is different, because you are prepared the way your stage director and coach wants you to be. I wanted it to be perfect, and it should have been. I'm angry at myself for not doing everything exactly right.

One Wednesday Mr. Rudolf called me down to his office to ask whether I would sing for them the following Saturday morning at ten thirty. He must have noticed how my eyes lighted up.

"It isn't anything special, Miss Peters," Mr. Rudolf said. "The fact is we are engaging a new assistant conductor on a scholarship. There are several applicants. We want to see how they accompany while someone is singing."

"Oh," I said.

"We'd like you to sing arias from *The Magic Flute, The Barber of Seville* and *Rigoletto*. We are also asking Paula Lenchner and Thomas Hayward. The chances are we will skip around a lot. Is that agreeable?"

"Why, of course," I said—without too much enthusiasm, I'm afraid.

"The judges will be Fritz Reiner, Fritz Stiedry, and myself."

That put an entirely different complexion on the matter.

Later that night, I summed it up in my diary: "It isn't anything big. But Reiner and Stiedry will be there. So, I'm going to sing exquisitely for them."

Again, on Saturday night I recorded the events of the day:

Reiner and Stiedry were smiling to Rudolf as I sang the second aria of the Queen of the Night. When I finished, Reiner applauded me and Stiedry said, "Wonderful!" After the auditions, Stiedry said he would like to hear me do some more. I sang the first aria of the Queen of the Night. Rudolf accompanied me. I did it very well. Rudolf played it in a truly Mozartian style.

As a modest afterthought, I added: "I was very pleased with the way I sang."

Midway in the course, I had a brief corridor encounter with Mr. Bing. The magazines and newspapers wanted to take pictures of some of the season's new singers, and we were asked to join Mr. Bing in the Woman's Club Room. Besides me, there were Marguerite Piazza, Genevieve Warner, Barbara

Troxell, and Lucine Amara. The photographer had us do all kinds of things. We acted, we sang, we posed with Mr. Bing. I wore my yellow shantung dress with a red scarf, and I was generally satisfied with myself. Then I went up to the costume room on the fourth floor and took two shots alone with Mr. Bing, as did Miss Piazza. I took both pictures wearing a gorgeous red velvet cape with ermine collar wrapped around me, the tailor kneeling beside me, taking measurements. I looked as if I were discussing the costume with Mr. Bing. Oh, it was fun! Afterward, as we walked down the corridor together, Mr. Bing suddenly asked, "Have you ever sung anywhere?"

Meekly I answered: "No, Mr. Bing."

"This isn't a bad place to start," he said.

To which I gushingly replied: "No one can be as thrilled as I!"

Wednesday morning, Mother woke me up bright and early to announce that the morning papers carried the names of the new singers. She didn't look too happy, however. I'll let my diary explain why:

> The *Times* has one of the pictures of the group. I look ghastly! The photographer said, "Has everyone wet their lips?" All smiled and I began to wet mine, and just then he took the picture. So I'm sticking my tongue out at Mr. Bing!

I was heartbroken. It was the very first time my picture had appeared in the papers. Naturally everyone teased me about it, and I spent the entire day stammering excuses. As partial consolation there was a line in *Variety* describing me as "a vocalistic dark horse and star potential." That gave me quite a lift.

The last week of the course overlapped with the opening week of the Metropolitan rehearsals for the new season. And the first thing I knew I was invited to attend the rehearsals of *Don Giovanni*. That was my cue. My instructions were to sit and watch Nadine Conner work in the role of Zerlina. I'm still required to do that. Even when I'm not scheduled to sing in a performance, I'm expected to sit in the auditorium and watch the rehearsals. The invitation comes on a little slip which is put in my mailbox. The wording is still the same: "Please report for rehearsal, on stage, auditorium, 10:30."

Which means that at ten-thirty on that particular day little Roberta Peters is going to be there, come what may.

A few days more and the Katherine Turney Long courses finally came to an end. They had been fun, after all, and I had been given a practical lesson in what I already could do and what I still had to do. From what I jotted down in my diary the last day of school, I gather I had completely changed my mind about "singing to the walls."

That night I wrote:

> I can proudly say that I haven't missed one lesson, not one, in the whole six weeks I have been doing this thing. I think I came through with flying colors. I worked in the house and got to know all the people down there. This in itself is a tremendous thing. First, because I got used to them and second, because they had a chance to see what I'm capable of doing.

That was Friday night, October 13, 1950. Roberta Peters, age twenty years and five months, was obviously feeling quite pleased with herself.

7

♦♦♦♦♦♦♦♦♦♦

Friday, November 17, 1950 . . .

Age: 20

I WOKE up at ten o'clock and my first thought was food; my second thought was that I couldn't have any.

"Darn it!" I said to myself "My metabolism test!"

I was due at the doctor's at eleven o'clock. I hadn't had dinner the night before and no lunch before that. And now I wasn't supposed to have breakfast.

Since I was sixteen years old, I have been checking regularly on my metabolism. At one time in my studies my voice was very low and misty and veiled, and Mr. Herman sent me to a doctor for a checkup.

"Thyroid deficiency," said the doctor. "I suggest you have a metabolism test every few months, just to be sure."

So the time had come for another visit to the doctor. I woke up good and hungry, though it wasn't till I was dressed that I began to feel unhappy about it. I wanted so much to have my two eggs and toast and coffee and orange juice.

Nonchalantly I slipped into the kitchen. Mother saw me.

"The doctor wouldn't like it, darling," she said, wagging a warning finger.

Mother had given up her job as milliner in a hat factory six months earlier. Dad was working as a salesman in a shoe store. He had left for work at eight-thirty.

I then weighed 117 pounds, which is what my weight usually is, a pound more or less. At 10:45 Mother and I took a cab to the doctor's office. I was feeling quite weak—I was famished.

When the cab stopped at West Ninety-fourth Street, where the office was located, Mother remained seated as I got out.

"I've got some shopping to do, Bobbie," she said. "I'll see you home between five and five thirty. Be careful."

I had walked a few steps when she called out after me: "Oh, and don't forget we have two places for *Don Giovanni* tonight. So let's eat dinner early."

Nadine Conner was scheduled to sing Zerlina that night. The curtain was for eight o'clock.

I said good-bye and went into the doctor's office. I proceeded with the preparations that are needed for the test. I rested for a half hour and the doctor made the first part of the check.

I ate the standard two hard-boiled eggs before taking the second part of the test. I can't recall when an egg tasted better.

Finally the doctor studied the lines and figures, made his calculations, and turned to me with a reassuring smile.

"It's as close to normal as it's ever been," he said; "almost at the zero point, in fact."

That made me feel good. It was now an hour since I had eaten the two eggs, and I was feeling hungrier than ever. The doctor then gave me a routine physical checkup.

"You're in perfect shape, young lady," he said. "Now run, don't walk, to the nearest restaurant."

I left the doctor's office at exactly one-thirty. In no time at all I was carrying out his orders at the lunch counter of Schrafft's at Broadway and Ninety-fourth Street.

"Two eggs and bacon and toast and coffee and a nice big piece of Danish pastry, please," I fairly shouted to the girl behind the counter.

She eyed me with amusement. We had chatted on previous visits, and she knew I was a singer.

"Somebody's been fasting," she said.

"I'll say," I replied. "Metabolism test. Only two hard-boiled eggs in twenty-four hours."

"How's the singing coming?"

I said, "Fine, fine—but right now all I can think of is food."

I was due at Mr. Herman's studio at three o'clock. It was now two. While I ate, I kept wondering how I would kill the hour. I decided a little walk might be just the thing.

Just as I was about to leave the restaurant, something told me to call Mr. Herman. I would often do that just to find out how he is. But, why at two in the afternoon, when I was to see him at three? I dialed the number.

I was feeling quite good, gloating over my feast, humming to myself snatches of the music of *Don Giovanni* that Mother and I were going to hear that evening. I heard Mr. Herman's voice say "Hello" at the other end.

I had barely chirped a blithe "How are you?" when out it came.

"Where the hell are you?" he shouted. "The doctor said you left his office an hour ago!"

He sounded frantic, as if the studio had just caved in over him. I was terrified.

"What's happened?" I shouted back.

"Never mind what's happened! Where are you?"

I told him.

"Well, get over here right away!" And he hung up before I could catch my breath.

I bustled out of the phone booth, out of Schrafft's, and into the first cab that came along. I fell back in my seat panting. I couldn't imagine what was up.

I expected to be greeted by a wild and angry Bill Herman when I arrived at the studio. Instead, he was quite calm—and serious. That's the way he is.

"Sit down, Roberta," he said gently.

I sat down, more mystified than ever, and more alarmed too. He came right to the point.

"The Metropolitan has been calling your home and my studio. . . ."

I said nothing, just stared at him, tense and expectant.

". . . There's an emergency."

"Oh!"

"You must get down there immediately."

"Did they say why?" I stammered.

That almost shattered his calm.

"They didn't tell me what it's about."

My mind leaped ahead to *The Magic Flute*. That was scheduled for the following day, Saturday. Maybe Erna Berger was ill and . . .

"It's for the Queen of the Night!" I exclaimed.

After all, that's the part I had been engaged for, and it was one of the Queen's arias that I had sung over and over again for them at my audition. . . .

"Possibly," said Mr. Herman impatiently. "But don't speculate. Just you get down there as fast as you can!"

So I went down to the Metropolitan. It was just one cab after another that day. You can imagine my state of mind, the suspense, the uncertainty, the sneaking feeling that this was it.

By the time I got to the Thirty-ninth Street entrance, I had quite made up my mind they were going to ask me to substitute the following day in *The Magic Flute*.

It could be something else, of course, maybe a new role, maybe even something bad. . . .

There wasn't the remotest suspicion in my mind that the emergency call might be for the same night.

The moment I entered, I felt it. It was in the atmosphere, in the looks on people's faces. I had suddenly become an important person.

Margaret Carson, the head of the press office, was all smiles as she jumped up to greet me.

"Mr. Bing is very anxious to see you," said Miss Carson, as if hugging a deep, dark secret.

The others looked up from their desks, smiling.

My heart pounding, I went into Mr. Bing's office. He got up to shake my hand.

"Miss Peters," he said, "an emergency has arisen. A rather grave one, in fact. One of our artists has fallen sick."

"I'm so sorry, Mr. Bing—I hope it isn't anything serious."

"It is serious—for us. I've called in my stage director and he assures me that he has every confidence that you can do the role."

So it *was* the Queen of the Night in *The Magic Flute,* and Erna Berger was ill! And I was being asked to step in the following day! That's what I thought. I was appalled.

"We want you to take over Nadine Conner's part as Zerlina in tonight's *Don Giovanni,*" said Mr. Bing.

"Tonight?" I blurted out, "In *Don Giovanni!*"

I went numb. Five hours from now! The long-awaited Metropolitan debut on such short notice! I was dreaming.

Mr. Bing was eyeing me silently, in a gentle but penetrating way.

"Of course, Mr. Bing," I found myself saying. "I'm sure I could do it."

"I know you can," he said. "Dr. Graf has told me that he

worked with you on the role at the school. He said you're absolutely ready."

"I'm so happy to know you have such confidence in me," I said.

Mr. Bing didn't seem to hear.

"See if you can get a costume to fit you and get home as fast as possible to rest up.... Oh, let's go in and see Mr. Rudolf before you go."

Mr. Rudolf looked pleased in a sly, impish way, when we entered his office. He began nodding his head in a curious way, in a kind of proud approval.

I must have looked dazed. All he said was:

"It will be all right, really; it will be all right."

He was like a father at that moment.

Just as I was leaving, Mr. Bing came over and kissed me on the forehead.

"Tell the taxicab driver to go slowly," he said. "He has a very precious cargo tonight. Nothing must happen to you."

We both laughed.

"Be back at seven," Mr. Rudolf called after me, "and go straight to Dr. Reiner's dressing room."

I rushed down the corridor. I was panting like mad as I came through Miss Carson's office again. She must have sensed the state I was in. We just flew into each other's arms.

My heart was pounding a mile a minute as she held me like a mother. I needed that moment's shelter and comfort in a woman's arms more than anything in the world. I was so moved, I almost cried.

"Just go home and get a good rest," she said. "It's wonderful news."

It was now about three-thirty.

I didn't listen to Mr. Bing or Miss Carson. Instead of going home, I took a cab to Mr. Herman's studio. When I got there,

he ushered me without a word into the studio and closed the
door behind us.

"I'm singing . . . tonight!"

I had never seen that look in his eyes—it was happiness,
shock, surprise, incredulity, all in one. It seemed to strike us
both at the same time, like a dream. Nothing had been farther
from our thoughts.

Suddenly we both laughed, and the strain broke. I laughed
till there were tears in my eyes. Then Mr. Herman was all
seriousness again.

"Are you up on the music?" he asked.

He wasn't worried about the stage action, about my voice;
he was only worried about whether I was sure of the music.
You see, neither of us had ever seriously considered the chance
that I might make my debut as Zerlina. I had studied the role,
and I had heard that Dr. Reiner was interested in hearing me
do it for him, but only for a possible audition. We had the
feeling that it would be a long time before they asked me to
sing it at the Met. Zerlina was just another role I knew I had
to learn.

"I think so, Mr. Herman," I said.

"Well, whether you think so or not, I think you'd better go
up to the library and go over whatever parts you're still leery
about with Henry."

Henry, of course, was our accompanist, Henry Smith, who
has been such a help in so many emergencies.

So up the stairs I flew to the third floor of Mr. Herman's
house. There was Henry at the piano, waiting. I told him my
news.

"Good work, Roberta!" he said, beaming.

"Thank you so much, Henry. I still can't believe it. . . . Mr.
Herman thinks we ought to go through the music of Zerlina."

"All set?"

"All set."

Mostly we worked on the ensembles. After a few minutes with Henry I knew there was nothing to worry about as far as the arias and duets were concerned.

But we went over the ensembles very carefully. I didn't want to mess anybody else up, just in case I fluffed a note when we were all singing together.

Henry and I worked till about four.

"I wish you the best of luck," he said. "I know you'll be fine."

It had been a short but reassuring session. Mr. Herman hadn't wanted me to work too hard for fear of tiring myself. As I got into my coat, he said, "Go home and try to rest. Henry and I will be over around six and we'll run through it all again before we leave for the Met."

I arrived at home at four-fifteen. For one solid hour I was all alone with the news of my debut! Mother was roaming from shop to shop somewhere downtown. There was no chance of getting the news to her. I couldn't remember the name of Dad's shoe store, and there was no trace of his telephone number in the house. It was the strangest and longest hour in my life. I tried to lie down and couldn't. I tried to sit and couldn't. There wasn't anyone to talk to but myself.

I went wandering about the apartment, humming little bits of *Don Giovanni*. I walked around chairs and tried to see myself on the stage: What I would do, where I would be, who would be where doing what. I was excited, restless, and everybody had told me to go home and relax! Relax!

Curiously, I never once thought of it as my chance, my great opportunity. During that strange hour I didn't even think of it as a job or assignment. Maybe I was in a sort of trance. I know I wasn't in the least scared. It was as if some power were guiding me, or rather taking care of everything for me. It was like a mission. As I look back, there was plenty to worry about, but somehow I couldn't worry. I knew I would be all right, and yet how easily I could have been wrong. I had nobody to talk to about it. Why didn't Mother come? Why didn't Dad call?

I was anxious, but only in this sense: I wanted to accomplish what was being asked of me. I knew I could do it. But I just couldn't wait!

Finally it was five-fifteen. The hour was up. I heard a key in the door and Mother walked in. I rushed up to her and said, "Sit down, Mother! I've got something to tell you!"

She looked frightened. Before she could open her mouth, I had literally dragged her to the couch and pushed her down, with all her bundles.

"What's the matter, Bobbie? The doctor! He found something wrong with you?"

I could have cried when I saw the look of concern on her face.

I gave her a big smile and broke the news.

"I'm singing tonight!"

It didn't sink in at first.

"But how can you? We've got tickets for the opera tonight!"

Suddenly it dawned on her. Her eyes opened wider than I've ever seen them. For a moment she sat there dazed and speechless.

"Not at the Metropolitan!"

"At the Metropolitan, darling!"

"But how, when . . . but I left you at the doctor's!"

"It's all very simple," I said, pretending to be casual. "Nadine Conner is sick, and Mr. Bing has asked me to sing Zerlina tonight. I told him I would."

Mother jumped up from the couch, threw all her parcels in the air, and gave a shriek of joy. She threw her arms about me. We were just in a state.

Suddenly I felt hungry again.

"How about a big juicy steak, Mom?"

She didn't seem to hear.

"Are you sure you'll be all right?"

"Not if you're going to starve me. Do I get a steak?"

"I'll start dinner right away. . . . But it's such short notice, Bobbie. . . ."

"For the dinner, Mom?" I teased.

"Oh, all right—but you'd better go in the bedroom and lie down."

I did. I tried to sleep, but that was out of the question. I could hear Mother bustling about in the kitchen, opening parcels, turning on the gas—all the pleasant sounds of food to come.

Then I heard her dialing. I knew she was phoning Dad and waited with her for his cry at the other end as she made the announcement. She hung up and came into the bedroom.

"I told Dad to meet us backstage," she said. "Not a chance —he's hurrying right over."

We both realized there was no point in my trying to lie down. In a few minutes the door opened and Dad, grinning like a child, came in. He came to me and hugged me, and I could feel in his voice that, like Mother, he was a little nervous too. In all that excitement neither of them ate a thing that night.

Promptly at six the doorbell rang, and Mr. Herman entered with Henry. After a quick exchange of greetings, Mother flew into the kitchen. Dad followed her, and Henry went over to the piano. My steak appeared right in the middle of one of Zerlina's melodies.

While Henry played the piano and Mr. Herman coached and Mother and Dad stood by watching and listening, I dug into my juicy steak.

I'd be chewing away and Mr. Herman would be saying, "Be careful at this phrase, it's tricky; it takes a lot of breath; try to conserve your breath as much as possible; it's a long phrase. . . . Are you following me?"

And I'd gulp down another mouthful of meat and vegetables.

"Yes, Mr. Herman. It's a long phrase and I should [swallow] conserve my breath. . . ."

"Let's have 'Batti, batti,' Henry."

And Henry would begin Zerlina's tender little aria and I'd hum or sing along between bites.

This went on till I finished my steak and vegetables. I swallowed my cup of tea and looked up to see the amused faces of Henry and Mr. Herman.

"You've got nothing to worry about," said Mr. Herman.

"Not with an appetite like that," said Henry.

Mother had meanwhile gone into the bedroom to lay out my clothes.

"I think you'd better get dressed, darling," she said. So I left Mr. Herman, Henry, and Dad, and began to dress for the trip downtown.

It was now six-forty P.M.

Mother had packed whatever makeup articles I had into a little traveling case. They weren't much—pancake makeup, rouge, eyebrow pencil. She stuffed a robe and slippers into the bag.

As we left the house, Mr. Herman hailed a cab and we all jumped in. And before we knew it, we were caught in one of the worst traffic snarls I can remember.

That corner of Broadway and Seventieth Street is ordinarily one of the busiest in town. But that night, of all nights of the year, it seemed to be busiest of all. Almost motionless traffic.

I would have sworn that all the trucks in the world had congregated there that evening. In addition, everybody in New York seemed to be returning home from work by that route.

There was no way of moving over all those cabs and trucks except by leaping over them. We were really stuck. So we all got a little nervous and fidgety and exasperated, especially Mr. Herman.

After what must have been five nerve-wracking minutes, he finally said: "This is silly! Let's take the subway. It's the safest way. At this rate we'll never get down there."

We got out and walked a block to the subway station at Broadway and Seventy-second Street. A downtown express was just pulling in, and within five minutes we were at the Metropolitan entrance at Fortieth Street and Seventh Avenue.

I took off my coat and handed it to Mother, who passed me my score. I left Mother, Dad, and Mr. Herman, and in double-quick time headed for Dr. Reiner's dressing room.

To get there I had to cross the full length of the Metropolitan stage. That gave me the strangest feeling. As I ran, I wondered what my fate would be a few hours later. The set of the first scene of *Don Giovanni* was already down. It seemed to be eyeing me, cautioning me....

I knocked timidly on Dr. Reiner's door. Mrs. Reiner opened it, and as I came in, she threw her arms about me. Dr. Reiner was all smiles. He gave me a warm handclasp.

"Don't worry about a thing," he said. "I'll watch over you."

"I'm so happy to be singing for you, Dr. Reiner . . ." I began.

"Let's go to the piano for a moment," he said. "I want to show you my tempi."

We did the arias, and then Dr. Reiner called in the evening's Don Giovanni, Paul Schoeffler, a big jolly fellow, with a wide grin.

"Now, suppose we go through the duet," said Dr. Reiner.

Mr. Schoeffler and I sang "La ci darem la mano."

"I'm very happy to meet my new Zerlina," said Mr. Schoeffler. "*Hals und Beinbruch!*"

That is the German stage term for "Good luck!" though you would never guess it from the literal meaning, which is just the opposite: "May you break your neck and legs!"

"Now go and get dressed," said Dr. Reiner. "Remember, I'll be keeping an eye on you."

I suddenly was elated in a strange new way. This wonderful man and musician had made me feel assured and comfortable. I rushed to my dressing room. Outside, waiting, were Mother, Dad, and Mr. Herman.

"Dr. Reiner says I'll be all right," I said.

They all looked as if they needed to be told that.

Inside, waiting for me, was that lovable backstage companion, Jenny Cervini, the wardrobe mistress.

It was comforting and strengthening to have her there at that moment. Jenny was sweet and gentle but professional and efficient. At a time like that it is important to have professional people around you.

As a rule, people who are emotionally involved should never be present on such an occasion. Their nervousness can be catching.

I must say Mother was wonderful, fully as businesslike and professional as Jenny. Only later did she confess to me that she was trembling with fear and anxiety. But she kept it all inside.

Dad was standing outside the dressing room with Mr. Herman, both nervous wrecks, I'm sure.

The curtain was for eight o'clock.

I was dressed by eight sharp, but wasn't scheduled to go on stage, in the order of scenes, till about eight-fifteen. I had nothing to do for fifteen minutes. I didn't know what to think. I didn't want to think. I was afraid I might get myself all tied up inside if I began thinking. I was just eager to get going.

At a minute or so to eight, Dad and Mr. Herman left their post in the corridor outside to go into the house.

At eight-thirteen there was a sharp knock on the door. It was the call-boy.

"Two minutes, Miss Peters!"

It almost caught me off my guard. My mind had just drifted and drifted, without conscious thought. . . .

I said, "Thank you."

Jenny turned to me and said:

"*In bocca lupo!*"

That is the Italian stage term for "Good luck!"—literally, "In the mouth of the wolf!"—a pleasant thought!

"*Mille grazie, cara!*" I said to Jenny, grasping her hand.

Finally I opened the door. Mother looked at me and I looked at her.

"Good luck," she said, "and may God bless you!"

"Good luck!" echoed Jenny.

And I walked out.

Epilogue

PETERS, Roberta, soprano, operatic singer; b. N.Y.C., May 4, 1930; d. Sol and Ruth (Hirsch) Peterman; ed. privately; m. Bertram Fields, Apr. 10, 1955; children—Paul, Bruce. Met. Opera debut as Zerlina in Don Giovanni, Nov. 1950, also appeared in Rigoletto, The Magic Flute, the Barber of Seville, The Marriage of Figaro, Lucia di Lammermoor, Die Fledermaus, Don Pasquale, L'Elisir d'Amore, Lakme, Cosi Fan Tutte, La Sonnambula, Martha, also appeared in Richard Strauss' Ariadne auf Naxos; recorded several operas; appeared motion picture Tonight We Sing; frequent appearances radio and TV; sang at Royal Opera House, Covent Garden, London, Eng., summers 1951-60; with Cin. Opera, summers 1952-53, 1958, Vienna State Opera, 1963, Salzburg Festival, 1963, 1964; debuts at festivals in Vienna and Munich, 1963, 1964; concert tours in U.S., Soviet Union, Scandinavian countries. Named Woman of Yr., Fedn. Women's Clubs, 1964. Home: Scarsdale, N.Y. Office: care Maurice Feldman, 551 Fifth Av., N.Y.C. 17.

Reproduced with the permission of Marquis-Who's Who, Inc., from the 34th edition of *Who's Who in America.*